Reading American History

Getting the Main Idea
Learning the Vocabulary
Reading Maps and Graphs

Glenn E. Hughes

Norman D. Miller

Stephen L. Volkening

Scott, Foresman and Company

Editorial Offices: Glenview, Illinois
Regional Offices: Sunnyvale, California • Atlanta, Georgia
Glenview, Illinois • Oakland, New Jersey • Dallas, Texas

Authors

Glenn E. Hughes, Reading Coordinator, Joliet Central High School, Joliet, Illinois
Norman D. Miller, Social Science Chairman, Joliet Central High School, Joliet, Illinois
Stephen L. Volkening, Social Science Teacher, Joliet Central High School, Joliet, Illinois

To our patient and understanding wives and children—Annette, Kay, Mary Jo, Amy, Bruce, Cheryl, Deanna, Erik, Kurt, Sarah, and Todd—we dedicate this book to you.

ISBN: 0-673-35159-9 Student's Edition

5678910-WEB-95

Table of Contents

How to Use the Book

Getting the Main Idea

When reading American history (or any other subject), you should be aware that the main idea of the paragraph can be located in several different places. Read the paragraph below and underline what you think is the main idea.

In 1650, Catholics and Quakers were severely punished if they entered the city of Boston. The first time a Catholic or a Quaker entered the city, one ear was cut off. If that person was found in the city a second time, the other ear was cut off. The tongue was pierced by a red-hot iron on the third time. As the years passed, laws punishing Catholics and Quakers became even more strict. The second time they entered the city, they were put to death by hanging.

In the paragraph above, the first sentence gives the main idea. The other sentences give more details about the main idea.

Read the next paragraph and underline what you think is the main idea.

After they were brought from Africa to America, slaves were sold at a slave auction. Many times, they were bought and sold like animals. They were put up on a platform to be viewed. Buyers made them jump up and down to test their strength. After they had been viewed for a while, the bidding was started. Slaves were sold to whoever offered the highest bid. Many times, families were broken up and sold to different masters. The auctions were usually very cruel experiences for the slaves.

In this paragraph, the main idea is found in the last sentence. This paragraph is thus developed in the opposite way of the first example. Here, the first few sentences give examples and details. These details are then summarized by the last sentence of the paragraph.

Read the next paragraph and underline what you think is the main idea.

Most people thought that Thomas Dewey, the Republican candidate, would win the presidential election in 1948. Even many of his fellow Democrats did not think Harry Truman had a chance. Some people placed the odds at fifteen to one in favor of Dewey. But Truman won the election in one of the biggest upsets in United States history. On election night, it had still seemed as though Dewey would win. One morning newspaper had already printed some papers announcing his victory. But then the final votes were counted. There is a famous photo of Truman holding a copy of the newspaper with the headline "Dewey Defeats Truman." Of course, Truman had a huge grin on his face.

In this last example, the main idea is found in the middle of the paragraph. The sentences at the beginning and the end of the paragraph all support the idea that Truman's victory was one of the biggest upsets in United States history.

In *Reading American History*, there are three different types of exercises on reading for the main idea. In the first type of exercise, you are asked to find the main idea of the paragraph by selecting the topic or key sentence. This, of course, is what you were asked to do in the three paragraphs above. Read the paragraph below and underline the sentence that best states the main idea.

The period between 1830 and 1860 could be called the Steamboat Age. Within ten years after the first successful steamboat was tested, steamboats were in use on the Great Lakes and on all major rivers across the country. They soon became the most important form of transportation. They could move goods quickly and cheaply. Steamboats were especially important because they could haul freight upstream against the current. By 1850, steamboats carried three times as many crops as were carried on railroads or canal boats.

In this paragraph, the first sentence should have been underlined. All the other sentences explain why the period between 1830 and 1860 could be called the Steamboat Age.

The second type of main idea exercise asks you to select the key idea from among three possible choices. After the paragraph, there are three sentences, lettered A, B, and C. You should be able to decide which of these three sentences best states the main idea of the paragraph. Then, write the letter of that sentence in the blank at the beginning of the paragraph.

_____ In the late 1800s, farmers faced many problems. The price they received for their crops dropped sharply. In 1867, farmers received more than $2.50 for a bushel of wheat. But ten years later, they were paid less than one dollar per bushel. Farmers were also hurt by natural disasters. Bad weather and insects often ruined their crops. Farmers had to pay the railroads high prices to ship their crops to market. Warehouses which stored the grain also charged high rates. When the farmers took out loans, the banks charged them high interest rates.

   A. Farmers received more money for their crops with each passing year.
   B. Farmers encountered many difficulties in the late nineteenth century.
   C. Railroads and banks charged the farmers very reasonable rates.

In this paragraph, sentence B best states the main idea. It is actually a restatement of the first sentence in the paragraph. All the other sentences in the paragraph explain the types of problems the farmers faced. Both sentence A and sentence C are false. Farmers received less, not more, for their crops each year. The last few sentences in the paragraph tell that railroads and banks charged high, not low, rates to farmers.

The final type of main idea exercise asks you to write out what you think is the main idea of the paragraph. Most times, the main idea of the paragraph is clearly stated. In some cases, however, the paragraph only hints or implies the main idea. You must then use hints or keys to determine the main idea. When you do this, you are making an inference. Read the paragraph below. Then write what you think is the main idea of the paragraph on the lines provided.

A "generation gap" developed between many parents and their children in the 1950s and 1960s. Parents and their teen-agers found that they had very little in common. Communication between adults and teen-agers became difficult. Parents were shocked by their children's clothing and hair styles. Many adults thought the music that young people listened to was just noise. Many teen-agers, in turn, often thought that their parents' music was "square." Their attitude was often one of "do your own thing." They rejected responsibility to enjoy a free life-style.

The main idea of this paragraph is _____

_____

The main idea of the above paragraph is that during the 1950s and 1960s many parents and their teen-age children found that they had little in common. This, of course, explains what a generation gap is. The rest of the paragraph gives examples.

Learning the Vocabulary

There are several methods that can be used to learn and remember vocabulary words. The method used in this book is the solving of various vocabulary games. The words used in the vocabulary are included in the main idea section.

The following are examples of the six types of vocabulary games in the book.

A. Completing the Sentence

Fill in the blank in the following sentence with the word that best fits.

Thomas Dewey   Harry Truman

1. _____ was elected President of the United States in 1948.

B. Matching the Word with Its Meaning

Match the vocabulary word on the left with the meaning on the right. Write the correct letter in the blank next to the vocabulary word.

_____ 1. Thomas Dewey   A. Person elected President of the United States in 1948

_____ 2. Harry Truman

C. Unscrambling the Nonsense Word

Unscramble the word in capital letters in the sentence. Write your answer in the blank.

1. **RARHY UMRTNA** was elected President of the United States in 1948.

1. _____

D. Filling in the Blanks

Read the sentence below. Then complete the sentence by filling in the spaces correctly. Each dash represents one letter in the correct spelling of the word.

1. _ _ _ _ _   _ _ _ _ _ _ was elected President of the United States in 1948.

E. Solving a Word Search Puzzle

The following word has been used in the main idea section. See if you can find this word in the word search puzzle. Circle it.

C   D   P   F   T   S   A   V   C   X   Z

H   A   R   R   Y   T   R   U   M   A   N

F   W   C   A   T   D   O   P   Q   C   A

F. Working a Crossword Puzzle: This game is self-explanatory.

The answer to all of the above games, in case there is any doubt, is Harry Truman.

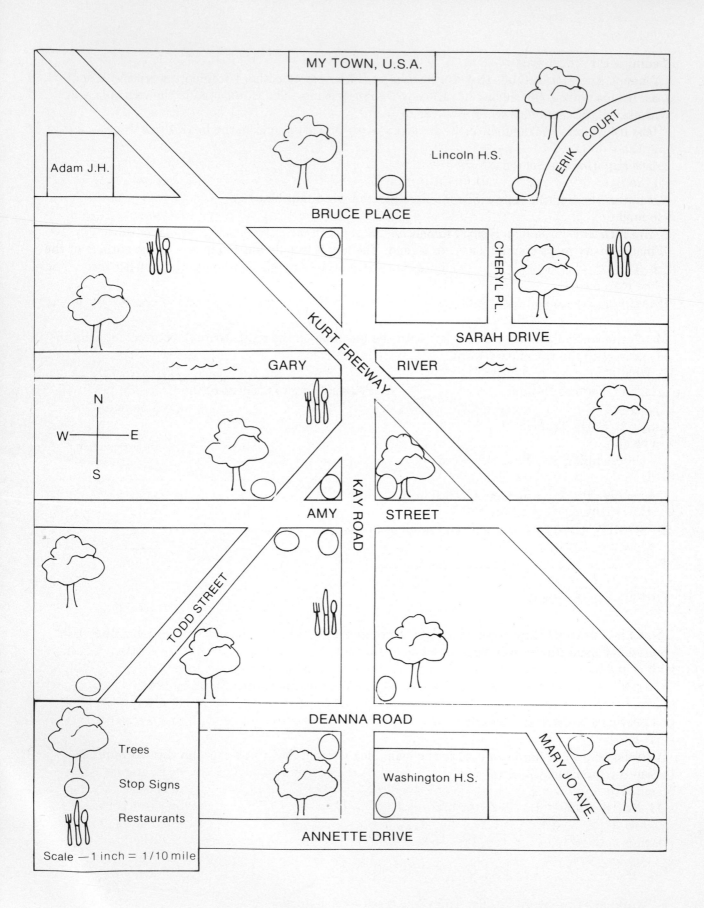

Reading Maps and Graphs

A map is a scaled-down version of something much larger. It shows the shape and relative size of areas. It may also show the location of such things as cities and bodies of water. While the content changes depending on the purpose of the map, many things are common to most maps.

Maps usually have a title. The title usually appears at the top of the page. Those few words tell you what the map is about.

Maps also show direction. Usually the top of the map is north, the bottom south, the left side west, and the right side east. Unless different instructions are given on a map, these directions are used.

Distance can also be shown on maps. Distances are drawn to scale. For example, one inch on the map might equal one mile on land. On such a map, a five-mile distance could be determined by measuring five inches. Thus, a map depicts something on paper in the same proportion as it exists in real life.

Finally, many maps contain a key, or legend. The key is usually located in one of the corners of the map. The key may be in shading or pictures or some other symbol. The key tells you what the symbols on the map mean.

See if you understand some of the features of a map by studying the map on the opposite page and then answering the questions below.

1. What is the title of this map? _____

2. If you turned off Deanna Road and headed for Amy Street on Kay Road, which direction would you be going? _____

3. How far is it from Bruce Place to Deanna Road? _____

4. How many restaurants are there on Sarah Drive? _____

5. How many stop signs are there on Todd Street? _____

Some information in American history is given in the form of charts and graphs. Line graphs are a particularly good way to show the increase or decrease of something. Since history is often concerned with changes over a period of time, line graphs are used most often in this book.

To read a line graph, you begin in the lower left corner. From that point, there are two things to locate. Up the left-hand side of the graph, there is a value. This is usually, but not always, a quantity of something. To the right in a horizontal position there is another value, usually in a steady progression. The progression is often expressed in units of time, but it can be something else.

In order for the graph to have any meaning, you must match the two values. In the example below, to find the number of tacos sold in March, you would look across the bottom of the graph to locate March. Then you would look up to find the dot above March. The dot shows the number of tacos sold. You determine what the number is by looking at the left side of the graph straight across from the dot. In this example, one finds that approximately 2,400 tacos were sold in March. The dot for March is connected to the dots for the other months by means of a line. By noting whether the line goes up or down, you can tell whether taco sales increased or decreased during the year.

See if you can answer the questions below the line graph that appears on the following page.

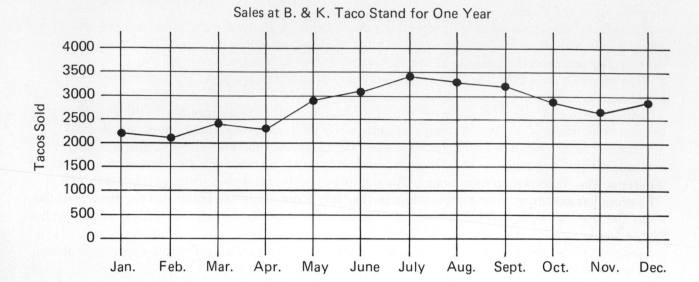

Sales at B. & K. Taco Stand for One Year

1. What do the numbers on the left side of the graph represent? _____

2. What is the information across the bottom of the graph? _____

3. In which month were sales highest? Approximately how many tacos were sold? _____

_____

4. In which month were sales lowest? Approximately how many fewer tacos were sold in that month

than in the month with the highest sales? _____

5. Which month experienced the sharpest increase from the previous month? _____

1 Reasons for Exploration

Getting the Main Idea

Read each paragraph below. Then write what you think is the main idea of each paragraph on the lines provided.

1. Before 1100, people in Europe knew little about the world around them. But then religious leaders sent out a series of armies to win back the Holy Land, the birthplace of Christ, from the Moslems. The wars these armies fought, which lasted over two hundred years, are called the crusades. The crusaders saw many strange new things in the Holy Land. They saw spices, jewels, dyes, and silks. They brought these goods back to Europe, where they became very popular. Spices were highly valued because they were used to cover up the taste of spoiled food in an age when people had no good way to preserve food. The demand for the goods brought back by the crusaders soon led to growing trade between Europe and Asia.

The main idea of this paragraph is _____

_____

2. Both of the two major trade routes between Europe and Asia were expensive and dangerous. The first route to Asia was by land across mountains and deserts. Travel was very slow over the bad roads. Traders had to pay high taxes when they passed through the lands of local princes. They were also often attacked by robbers. The second route was across the Mediterranean Sea. Travel by ship was slow too. It was also dangerous. Poor weather conditions could slow down or even sink the ships. Ships were sometimes attacked by pirates.

The main idea of this paragraph is _____

_____

3. As trade between Europe and Asia grew after the crusades, Italian merchants quickly took control of the water route across the Mediterranean to Asia. For nearly two hundred years, this gave the Italian cities of Genoa and Venice a monopoly over trade with Asia. This meant that the goods from Asia that were so highly prized in Europe entered only Italian seaports. Anyone who wanted spices or other riches from Asia had to buy them from an Italian merchant.

The main idea of this paragraph is _____

_____

4. The Italians made a lot of money on their trade with Asia. Goods from the East were sold at many times their price in Europe. If the Italians raised the price of any product, people in other European countries had no choice but to pay the higher price. They soon got tired of having their money enrich Italy. Other countries wanted to find a new route to Asia that was not in the hands of Italy. Explorers from Portugal and Spain set out to search for a new water route to Asian riches.

The main idea of this paragraph is _____

_____

2 Aids to Exploration

Getting the Main Idea

Read each paragraph below. Choose which of the three sentences following each paragraph best states the main idea of that paragraph. Write the letter of that sentence in the blank.

_____ 1. The early explorers faced many dangers. Their ships were unseaworthy. They often sank during bad storms at sea. The maps used by the sailors were often not very accurate. The sailors had to rely on landmarks. At night or when it was foggy, they could become lost. Because their ships were also small, they could not carry many supplies. When the food ran out, some of the sailors starved to death. Unsanitary conditions and poor diet also spread diseases among the crew. The explorers could not afford to hire the best sailors. Many times, sailors were recruited from prisons. They might mutiny aboard the ship.
  A. Sailors were very useful to the explorers.
  B. Explorers had many problems on their voyages.
  C. Using landmarks was an accurate method of navigation.

_____ 2. The invention of two navigation aids helped sailors sail across the oceans. One new aid was the compass. It was invented by the Chinese. The compass made it possible for sailors to find their direction no matter what the weather was like. The other navigation aid was the astrolabe. The astrolabe was used to measure the height of the sun. It told the sailors their latitude.
  A. The Chinese invented the astrolabe.
  B. The compass measured the height of the sun.
  C. The compass and astrolabe greatly helped the explorers navigate.

_____ 3. Prince Henry of Portugal did more than any other person to help find a new water route to Asia. He became known as the father of navigation. Henry built an observatory and school on the southwestern tip of Portugal. There, sailors studied the stars and learned to use the compass and astrolabe. Henry collected maps and charts of the world's oceans. He worked with shipbuilders to improve the design of ships. Henry also sent trained pilots on voyages along the coast of Africa. Henry died before their explorations were finished. But Bartholomew Diaz sailed as far as the Cape of Good Hope at the southern tip of Africa. Ten years later, Vasco da Gama sailed around Africa and across the Indian Ocean to India. An all-water route to Asia had been found.
  A. Henry of Portugal helped early explorers in many ways.
  B. Bartholomew Diaz was the father of navigation.
  C. Most of the earliest explorers were Spanish.

_____ 4. As exploration continued, Spain and Portugal began to compete over the newly discovered lands. Pope Alexander wanted to put an end to their disagreements. He settled the matter in 1493 by issuing the Bull of Demarcation. He divided the world in half with an imaginary line. This line was three hundred miles west of the Cape Verde Islands. Spain would be given all the newly discovered lands west of the line. Portugal would receive all new lands east of the line. When the line was drawn, the Old World of Europe did not know about the New World of North and South America. These lands were located in Spain's zone.
  A. Spain was given both the Old World and the New World.
  B. The Bull of Demarcation settled the rival claims of Spain and Portugal.
  C. Portugal was given all newly discovered lands west of the Cape Verde Islands.

3 Early Exploration

Getting the Main Idea

Read each paragraph below. Choose which of the three sentences following each paragraph best states the main idea of that paragraph. Write the letter of that sentence in the blank.

_____ 1. Christopher Columbus believed that the world was round. This belief was rejected by most sailors but accepted by many scientists at that time. Since the world is round, Columbus reasoned, he could reach Asia by sailing west. Sponsored by Spain, Columbus set sail from Spain in 1492 to find a new route to Asia. After a voyage of several months, he reached what he thought were the Spice Islands of Asia. Actually, Columbus was very lost. Instead of landing in Asia, Columbus really was in the Caribbean islands off the coast of North America. Columbus never knew that he had found a new continent.
  A. Columbus left Spain in 1492 to discover the New World.
  B. Columbus landed in North America in 1492 without ever knowing that he had found a new continent.
  C. All explorers knew that the world was flat.

_____ 2. Most people think that Columbus was the first person to discover America. This is not true. Both the Indians and the Vikings arrived before Columbus. Many thousands of years before Columbus was born, a group of people from Asia followed animal herds across a narrow strip of land that once connected North America to Asia. These people were the ancestors of present-day native Americans. About the year 1000, Leif Ericson, a Norwegian, led a group of Vikings to the east coast of North America. Because so many wild grapes grew there, they called the new land Wineland. They had rediscovered what the Indians had found long ago.
  A. Columbus was the first person to discover America.
  B. The Vikings reached America before the Indians.
  C. Both the Vikings and Indians reached America before Columbus.

_____ 3. In 1519, Ferdinand Magellan set out with five ships to sail around the world. The sailors aboard one of the ships mutinied. The sailors on two other ships deserted and returned home. The remaining sailors soon ran out of food and had to eat the rats on the ships. They narrowly escaped an attack by pirates in the Moluccas, islands that are now part of Indonesia. Magellan himself was killed by natives in the Philippines. Only one ship and eighteen sailors returned. Though the three-year voyage of Magellan's ship had been filled with dangers, it had finally proved that the world was round and that the Americas were a New World.
  A. Although it was dangerous, Magellan's voyage around the world was important.
  B. Magellan was killed by pirates in the Molucca Islands.
  C. Most of Magellan's crew were cowards.

_____ 4. Two explorers and soldiers of fortune named Hernando Cortés and Francisco Pizarro helped Spain set up a huge empire in the New World. Cortés fought and conquered the Aztecs of Mexico between 1519 and 1522. Pizarro conquered the Incas of Peru in 1533. Spain in time controlled all of South America (except Brazil), Central America, the West Indies, Florida, California, and the southwest part of America. Huge amounts of gold and silver were mined and shipped back home to Spain. For many years, its colonies in the New World made Spain the richest and most powerful country in the world.
  A. Cortés conquered the Incas, and Pizarro conquered the Aztecs.
  B. The Indians easily defeated the Spanish explorers.
  C. Its New World colonies made Spain rich and powerful.

4 Settlements in the New World

Getting the Main Idea

Read each paragraph below. Choose which of the three sentences following each paragraph best states the main idea of that paragraph. Write the letter of that sentence in the blank.

_____ 1.   The French got along very well with the Indians. The French were mainly fur trappers. They settled along the lakes and rivers in the interior of America and Canada. They did not try to take over the land where the Indians lived. They also did not cut down the trees to begin farming. The French sometimes lived with the Indians. They learned the Indians' language, ate Indian food, and dressed like the Indians. Sometimes, they married Indian women.
  A. The French trappers got along well with the Indians.
  B. The Indians tried to copy the French dress and language.
  C. French settlers in America were usually farmers.

_____ 2.   The Spanish colonies in the New World were ruled by a viceroy who was appointed by the king. The viceroy had complete power over life in the colonies. He carried out the laws, collected taxes, and controlled the trade. He also rewarded his friends with large amounts of land or gold. His enemies were severely punished. Under such a powerful government, the people in the Spanish colonies had almost no voice.
  A. Spanish viceroys were elected by the colonists in the New World.
  B. The viceroys ruling the Spanish colonies of the New World had complete power.
  C. The viceroy system soon made Spain lose its power and wealth.

_____ 3.   In 1614, the first Dutch settlers landed in what today is New York and New Jersey. To get more people to come to New Netherland, as their colony in the New World was known, the Dutch began the patroon system. The title of patroon was given to anyone who would bring fifty settlers to New Netherland. The patroon was given a large estate in return. The patroon gave the people a home, tools, animals, and seeds. When the crops were harvested, the settlers gave part of the harvest to the patroon.
  A. The Spanish easily conquered the Dutch by using the patroon system.
  B. The Dutch settlers were happy with the patroon system.
  C. The Dutch started the patroon system to bring more settlers to New Netherland.

_____ 4.   The first permanent English settlement in North America was founded in Jamestown, Virginia, in 1607. From the very beginning, the people of Jamestown faced a very difficult life. Jamestown was located near a swamp. Many settlers died of malaria carried by mosquitoes living in the swamp. Most of the people spent their time searching for gold or a water route to Asia. They planted only a few crops. When winter came, there was little food left. Winter became known as the "starving time." Other people were killed by Indians. Under such terrible conditions, fights often broke out, and still more people were killed. Over half the population of Jamestown died from one cause or another during the first six months.
  A. The Jamestown settlement was a great success in its first year.
  B. The Indians showed the English settlers at Jamestown a route to Asia.
  C. The settlers at Jamestown faced terrible living conditions.

5 English Colonies

Getting the Main Idea

Read each paragraph below. Then write what you think is the main idea of each paragraph on the lines provided.

1. In the early days in the English colonies, there were many jobs but not enough workers. At the same time, many people in England could not find work. Some of them heard that there were jobs in the New World. While they were eager to start a new life, they did not have enough money to pay for their fare to America. A system of indentured servants was started to take care of both these problems. Men and women signed contracts agreeing to work for a master for a certain period of time. The master would then pay for their trip to the New World. When the contract was over, the servants were given their freedom.

The main idea of this paragraph is _____

_____

2. At one time in England, all people were required to belong to the Church of England. Several groups were persecuted because they did not agree with the teachings of the Church. They were fined or put in jail. One group was the Pilgrims. They wanted to form their own church and have their own religion. Another group was the Society of Friends, better known as the Quakers. Since they believed that all people were equal before God, they refused to take their hats off when the king passed. They also believed that war was sinful and refused to join the army. Both the Pilgrims and later the Quakers finally moved to the New World to find freedom of religion.

The main idea of this paragraph is _____

_____

3. Many settlers in the New World faced diseases, fires, Indian raids, bad weather, and poor harvests. For a short period of time, the people in the small village of Salem in Massachusetts Bay Colony blamed all these problems on the devil. They believed that the devil was trying to drive them from their homes. They began to accuse certain people of being responsible for their hard life. They thought these people were witches. During the Salem Witchcraft Trials of 1692, over two hundred people were tried for being witches. Of these, nineteen were found guilty and hanged. One old man was tortured to death for refusing to testify at his trial.

The main idea of this paragraph is _____

_____

4. Slaves in both the Spanish and Portuguese colonies were treated better than slaves in the English colonies. They were protected by law. They were allowed to marry and attend church. Harsh punishment was forbidden. Slaves in the English colonies, on the other hand, were thought of as chattel. This meant that they belonged to someone else. They had no legal or social rights.

The main idea of this paragraph is _____

_____

6 Exploration

Learning the Vocabulary

Fill in the blank in each of the following sentences with the word that best fits. Use each word in the list below just once.

Henry of Portugal   Indians
Ferdinand Magellan   Bull of Demarcation
Hernando Cortés   Bartholomew Diaz
Vasco da Gama   Francisco Pizarro
Christopher Columbus   Vikings

1. The _____ landed on the eastern shore of North America about 1000 A.D.

2. The famous prince who became known as the father of navigation was _____

    _____ .

3. _____ landed in America in 1492.

4. Pope Alexander issued the _____ to settle the rival land claims of

    Spain and Portugal.

5. The voyage of _____ proved that the world was round.

6. The _____ really discovered America thousands of years before Columbus.

7. _____ was the first European explorer to reach the Cape of Good

    Hope at the southern tip of Africa.

8. _____ was the explorer who proved that there was an all-water

    route to Asia.

9. The Aztecs of Mexico were conquered by _____ .

10. _____ defeated the Incas of Peru.

7 People and Places

Learning the Vocabulary

The following words have been used in the main idea section. See if you can find these words in the word search puzzle below. Circle the words. They may be found vertically or horizontally. They may also overlap.

crusaders
New World
Old World
Holy Land
New Netherland
Jamestown
Pope Alexander
Magellan

indentured servant
Henry of Portugal
Vikings
Indians
Pilgrims
Quakers
Aztecs
Incas

```
H  E  N  R  Y  O  F  P  O  R  T  U  G  A  L  C  D
O  T  E  M  C  B  T  V  I  K  I  N  G  S  C  W  F
L  V  W  C  M  C  W  R  D  N  L  O  A  G  D  P  W
Y  O  W  J  A  M  E  S  T  O  W  N  J  A  A  O  C
L  C  O  F  G  F  C  Q  T  V  L  D  O  M  Z  P  X
A  B  R  W  E  Q  U  A  K  E  R  S  C  N  T  E  Y
N  D  L  X  L  C  Z  N  L  A  M  F  S  G  E  A  L
D  R  D  O  L  X  U  S  D  D  N  O  I  O  C  L  M
F  W  D  Q  A  V  W  D  I  N  D  I  A  N  S  E  C
B  R  S  V  N  L  X  B  F  A  O  T  T  T  V  X  F
I  P  I  L  G  R  I  M  S  F  O  C  I  N  C  A  S
I  N  D  E  N  T  U  R  E  D  S  E  R  V  A  N  T
N  E  W  N  E  T  H  E  R  L  A  N  D  G  F  D  Q
X  U  O  Y  C  N  O  L  D  W  O  R  L  D  U  E  O
Q  C  R  U  S  A  D  E  R  S  G  T  O  I  X  R  P
```

8 Settlement

Learning the Vocabulary

Unscramble the words in capital letters in each of the sentences below. Write your answers in the blanks at the bottom of the page.

1. The Society of Friends, better known as the **KAQUERS,** came to America so they could follow their own religion.

2. The **GLIPIRSM** also came to America to find religious freedom.

3. Slaves were called **AHTCELT** because they were considered property and had no legal rights.

4. Twenty people were killed in 1692 as a result of the **MEALS TWIFATCRCH STRLAI.**

5. An **INEDNTDERU VRESTNA** signed a contract to work a certain period of time for a master who would pay for his or her trip to America.

6. **NWTOSEMJA** was the first permanent English settlement in the New World.

7. The **SIDNANI** settled in America long before the Vikings or Columbus arrived.

8. The **RCHENF** were mainly fur trappers and got along well with the Indians.

9. Gold and silver from its colonies made **APINS** the richest and most powerful country in the world for many years.

10. The Dutch used the **NOROTAP** system to encourage more people to come to New Netherland.

1. _____

2. _____

3. _____

4. _____

5. _____

6. _____

7. _____

8. _____

9. _____

10. _____

9 People, Places, and Things

Learning the Vocabulary

Fill in the squares to spell out the names or terms described in the clues.

ACROSS
3. Point on the southern coast of Africa first reached by the explorer Bartholomew Diaz
7. Aid to navigation that was used to measure the height of the sun
9. Powerful rulers of the Spanish colonies

DOWN
1. Aid to navigation invented by the Chinese that enabled sailors to find their direction no matter what the weather was like
2. Goods from Asia that were highly prized because they covered up the taste of spoiled food
3. Series of armies sent out from Europe to win back the Holy Land from the Moslems

4. Title given to any person who could bring fifty settlers to the Dutch colony of New Netherland
5. Country that controlled the water trade route between Asia and Europe for almost two hundred years
6. Pope who settled the rival land claims of Spain and Portugal by dividing the world in half with an imaginary line
8. Portuguese prince who built an observatory and school, collected maps of the world's oceans, and worked with builders to improve the design of ships

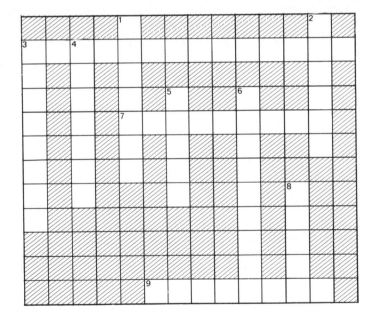

10 Voyages of Discovery

Reading Maps and Graphs

Study the map below about some of the early voyages of discovery. Then answer the questions that follow.

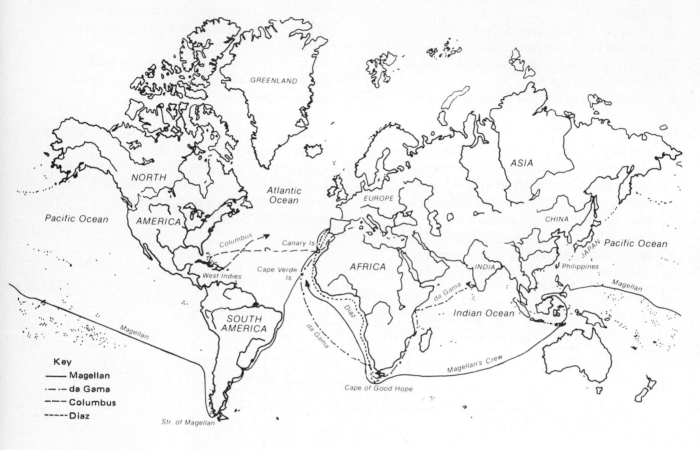

1. Which explorer ended his voyage at the Cape of Good Hope? _____

2. Which explorer reached India? _____

3. Which explorer reached the West Indies? _____

4. Which voyage went around the world? _____

5. In what general direction did Magellan sail? _____

11 North American Possessions, 1663

Reading Maps and Graphs

Study the map on European possessions in North America in 1663. Then answer the questions. Compare this map with a present-day map of North America, if necessary.

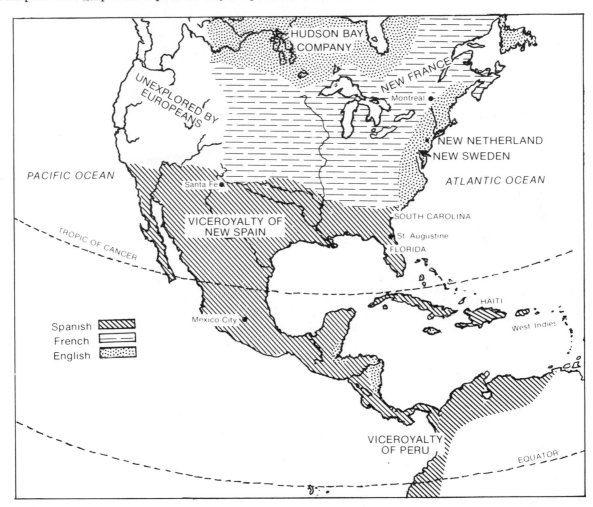

1. What five European countries are shown holding land in North America in 1663? _____

_____

2. Which two countries had the smallest holdings in North America? _____

_____

3. Which country held the most territory in what is now the United States? _____

4. Which country had colonies that are farther north? _____

5. Which country held the most land between the Tropic of Cancer and the equator? _____

12 Colonial Trade Routes

Reading Maps and Graphs

Much of the trade during the colonial period was triangular, or three-cornered. One country would ship goods to a second country. That country would then ship other goods to a third country. It, in turn, would ship goods to the first country. Study the map showing two examples of triangular trade and answer the questions.

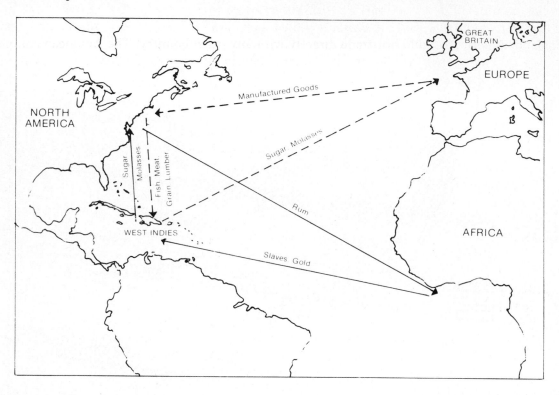

1. What areas are involved in the triangular trade route indicated by the solid line? _____

_____

2. What areas are involved in the trade route indicated by the dotted line? _____

_____

3. What products did the West Indies receive from these two trade routes? _____

_____

4. What product was sent from North America to Africa? _____

5. In what direction did ships carrying goods from the West Indies to Great Britain travel? _____

_____

1 Reasons for the Revolution

Getting the Main Idea

Read each paragraph below. Then underline the sentence that best states the main idea of each paragraph.

1. England used a plan known as mercantilism to keep it rich and strong. According to this plan, a country becomes rich by selling more goods to other countries than it buys from them. England applied this plan to the American colonies. It passed many laws forcing the colonies to buy goods only from England. Americans could not trade directly with any other country. The American colonies came to depend on England for everything. Mercantilism thus prevented the American colonies from becoming as strong and as rich as they might have been.

2. In the French and Indian War from 1754 to 1763, England and the American colonies fought together against France for control of the Ohio Valley. Winning the war put England in debt. People there were already paying high taxes to cover the costs of the war. They believed that the Americans should pay their share of the costs. Thus, after the French and Indian War, England increased its taxes on the American colonies.

3. In 1765, England passed the Stamp Act. This law required Americans to pay a tax on all printed materials such as newspapers, playing cards, and wills. The American colonists did not like the Stamp Act. They organized against it. Groups called the Sons of Liberty were formed to encourage people to resist the Stamp Act. Some colonists beat up the English tax collectors. Others burned the hated stamps. A very popular method of protest was the boycott. This means that the people refused to buy anything made in England until the tax was removed.

4. To escape paying the growing number of English taxes, some Americans took up smuggling. They illegally brought in goods made in other countries without paying any taxes on them. England tried to stop the Americans from smuggling by using writs of assistance. Today these writs of assistance would be called search warrants. A present-day search warrant, however, must say what is being searched for and where it is being looked for. In colonial times, the English tax collectors used writs of assistance to search any home or business for any kind of goods.

5. In 1770, five American civilians were accidentally killed by English soldiers in what became known as the Boston Massacre. As had happened many times before, a crowd of people gathered outside the tax collector's house in Boston. The crowd was protesting the English taxes. The people became very noisy. English soldiers were called out to guard the building. The captain tried to quiet the crowd and ordered the people to go home. The Americans called out insults and began throwing rocks and snowballs at the English soldiers. In the confusion, someone gave the order to fire. The soldiers shot into the crowd. When the smoke cleared after the shooting, three were dead, and two others were fatally wounded. One of the dead was a black sailor who had been the leader of the crowd.

2 Moving Toward Independence

Getting the Main Idea

Read each paragraph below. Then write what you think is the main idea of each paragraph on the lines provided.

1. For many years, the American colonists thought of themselves as citizens of England who happened to live in the New World. They obeyed English laws and paid English taxes. After a number of years, however, some people grew tired of being ruled by England. These people, known as rebels or Patriots, began to think of themselves as Americans. They thought Americans should be allowed to make their own laws rather than obey laws made in England. They also wanted to pass their own taxes instead of paying taxes to England. These American rebels began to demand independence from England.

The main idea of this paragraph is _____

_____

2. In 1774, delegates from all of the American colonies except Georgia met at the Continental Congress in Philadelphia. At the Continental Congress, the colonies acted together for the first time to demand that England restore their liberties. The members of the Continental Congress agreed that only the colonial governments, not England, had the right to pass taxes on the American colonies. They wanted to remove all the English taxes passed since the end of the French and Indian War in 1763. The members also agreed to boycott English goods until those taxes were ended. Committees were set up to see that the boycott was carried out.

The main idea of this paragraph is _____

_____

3. The Revolutionary War between the American colonies and England began at the Battle of Lexington in 1775. Several months before the battle, the colonists had been preparing for war. Bands of "minutemen" were ready to meet at a minute's notice to stop an attack by the English. On April 18, 1775, English soldiers tried to march into Lexington, Massachusetts, to seize the minutemen's supplies. The minutemen gathered to stop the English. Shots were fired by both sides. The war had begun.

The main idea of this paragraph is _____

_____

4. Even after the war broke out, many colonists remained loyal to the English king. More than one-half million people did not want to break away from England. These colonists called themselves Loyalists. But the rebels (Patriots) called them Tories. Many Tories fought on the English side. The rebels felt that the Tories were traitors. The Loyalists did not agree. They felt that the Patriots were the traitors.

The main idea of this paragraph is _____

_____

3 People of the Revolution

Getting the Main Idea

Read each paragraph below. Then write what you think is the main idea of each paragraph on the lines provided.

1. During the early years of the Revolutionary War, Benedict Arnold fought on the American side. A brave general, he played a key role in several important battles. But after a while, he became unhappy. He believed that he was not being promoted fast enough. Arnold also had money problems at home. Whatever his reason, in 1780 he made plans to surrender the fort at West Point which he commanded. He began to receive money from an English general. The plot, however, was discovered. Arnold was forced to flee West Point for the safety of an English ship. For the rest of the war, he fought for the English. Arnold thus became the most famous traitor in United States history.

The main idea of this paragraph is _____

_____

2. Haym Salomon was an American businessman who used his money and experience to help America win its independence from England. He loved freedom and worked all his life to win it. As a young man in Poland, Salomon fought in an unsuccessful war for Polish independence. When he moved to America, he soon began working for independence from England. His business made him very rich. He used much of his own money to buy goods for the American army. He used his business experience to help the new American government work out loans and trade agreements with France. Salomon also found people willing to loan money to the American government.

The main idea of this paragraph is _____

_____

3. Samuel Adams did more than any other American to bring about the Revolutionary War. Adams wrote articles about how unfairly the English treated the American colonies. He also made speeches urging people to organize against English rule. One of the founders of the Sons of Liberty, Adams led many demonstrations against the English taxes. He played a key role in the boycott of English goods. He also led the Boston Tea Party. In this protest over the high taxes on tea, American rebels dressed as Indians boarded English ships and threw their cargo of tea into the harbor.

The main idea of this paragraph is _____

_____

4. The Declaration of Independence was written chiefly by Thomas Jefferson. In it, Jefferson stated that people had the right to overturn any government which did not protect their rights of life, liberty, and the pursuit of happiness. He listed twenty-seven complaints against King George III of England. These wrongs had not been corrected. Jefferson concluded that the thirteen American colonies had no choice but to break their ties with England. When the Declaration was signed on July 4, 1776, the United States of America was born.

The main idea of this paragraph is _____

_____

4 The Revolutionary War

Getting the Main Idea

Read each paragraph below. Choose which of the three sentences following each paragraph best states the main idea of that paragraph. Write the letter of that sentence in the blank.

_____ 1. When the Revolutionary War broke out between England and the American colonies, England had many military advantages over the colonies. The English army was large and well trained. The American army was small and poorly organized. England had the most powerful navy in the world. The colonies had no navy at all when the war began. They had only privately owned ships, which had permission to attack the enemy. England had factories to make all the military supplies it needed. The colonies had few such supplies. England also was much better able to raise money to pay for the cost of the war than were the Americans.
  A. America's large army made it possible to win the Revolutionary War.
  B. The American army was larger and better trained than the English army.
  C. England had many military advantages over the colonies at the beginning of the war.

_____ 2. American blacks fought on both the American and the English sides from the very beginning of the Revolutionary War. Within a year, however, slaves and free blacks were no longer allowed to join the American side. George Washington, general of the American army, was afraid that slave owners in the South would be angry if their slaves ran off to fight. Then England began recruiting blacks by promising them their freedom after the war was over. This persuaded the colonies to allow blacks to serve in the American army again.
  A. Blacks fought on both sides in the Revolutionary War.
  B. More blacks fought on the American side than on the English side.
  C. When the Revolutionary War began, most blacks fought for the English.

_____ 3. During the Revolutionary War, most soldiers feared their doctors more than the enemy. Medical care at that time was very poor. If a soldier was shot in the arm, the doctor would cut it off. The wounded were not given anything to kill the pain during an operation. Most patients bled to death during or after an operation. At that time, doctors did not know about germs. Wounds were never cleaned out, and bandages were rarely changed. Under these conditions, many soldiers died of infection. Disease and poor medical care killed more soldiers than did enemy bullets.
  A. During the Revolutionary War, soldiers were given excellent medical care.
  B. More soldier died from disease and poor medical care than from enemy bullets during the Revolutionary War.
  C. American soldiers were cowards.

_____ 4. The Battle of Saratoga in 1777 was an important turning point of the war for the American colonies. The English planned to divide the colonies in half by gaining control of the Hudson River Valley. The American victory at Saratoga stopped this plan. It showed Americans that they might be able to win the war. The victory also impressed the king of France. After the battle, France joined the American side. France sent in needed supplies to the colonial army. French soldiers were sent in to fight against the English. The French navy also fought the English navy off the American coast.
  A. France signed a treaty to help England after the Battle of Saratoga.
  B. The Battle of Saratoga was an important American victory.
  C. England easily defeated America at the Battle of Saratoga.

5 The Articles of Confederation

Getting the Main Idea

Read each paragraph below. Choose which of the three sentences following each paragraph best states the main idea of that paragraph. Write the letter of that sentence in the blank.

_____ 1. When England signed the Treaty of Paris in 1783, the Revolutionary War was officially ended. England agreed that the United States was a free and independent country. Until then, England had felt that the American colonies were only part of the English empire in rebellion. In the treaty, England agreed to remove all its soldiers from the United States. Both sides agreed to free any prisoners captured during the war. England gave the United States full fishing rights off the Newfoundland coast. Most importantly, the Treaty of Paris set the boundaries of the United States. The boundaries were the Atlantic Ocean on the east, the Mississippi River on the west, the Great Lakes on the north, and Florida on the south.
  A. The Treaty of Paris ended the Revolutionary War with an English victory.
  B. After the Treaty of Paris, England still considered the United States part of its empire.
  C. When England signed the Treaty of Paris, it agreed that the United States was a free country.

_____ 2. When America broke away from English rule in 1776, its leaders knew they would have to learn to rule themselves. A plan for a new government was suggested in 1776. Known as the Articles of Confederation, this plan was first voted on in 1777. It was finally approved by the last state in 1781. From 1781 to 1788, the Articles of Confederation served as the basis for the American government.
  A. After the United States gained its freedom from England, it was afraid to rule itself.
  B. The Articles of Confederation acted as the basis for the American government from 1781 until 1788.
  C. England wrote the Articles of Confederation to rule the United States after 1776.

_____ 3. The writers of the Articles of Confederation did not want to give the new government too much power. The United States had just won a war with the powerful English king. Most Americans did not want to create a government of their own that would become too strong. Each of the thirteen states wanted to rule itself. The states wanted to make their own laws and solve their own problems. They did not want a strong government telling them what to do. Thus, the Articles of Confederation established a national government with very little power. The states kept most of the power for themselves.
  A. The United States patterned its new government after the English model.
  B. Under the Articles of Confederation, the national government was very powerful.
  C. The states had most of the power under the Articles of Confederation.

_____ 4. One of the good things that the new government did under the Articles of Confederation was to pass laws to govern the western lands won from England. The Land Ordinance of 1785 was one of the laws passed. Under this law, western lands were to be surveyed and divided into townships. Another important law was the Northwest Ordinance of 1787. It provided government for the western lands. It also set up a pattern by which this territory would in time enter the Union as new states with the same rights as the original thirteen states. The law further outlawed slavery in this territory.
  A. Under the Articles of Confederation, the government did some good things for the western lands.
  B. Slavery was allowed in all parts of the United States.
  C. The Northwest Ordinance provided that the western lands be surveyed.

6 Revolutionary War Terms

Learning the Vocabulary

Match the vocabulary words on the left with the meanings on the right. Write the correct letter in the blank next to the vocabulary word.

_____ 1. rebel

_____ 2. Stamp Act

_____ 3. Haym Salomon

_____ 4. Benedict Arnold

_____ 5. Northwest Ordinance

_____ 6. French and Indian War

_____ 7. writ of assistance

_____ 8. Battle of Lexington

_____ 9. Samuel Adams

_____ 10. minutemen

_____ 11. Thomas Jefferson

_____ 12. Articles of Confederation

_____ 13. Battle of Saratoga

_____ 14. Tory

_____ 15. George Washington

_____ 16. Declaration of Independence

_____ 17. Boston Tea Party

_____ 18. Sons of Liberty

_____ 19. Boston Massacre

_____ 20. Revolutionary War

A. First battle of the Revolutionary War
B. Groups of colonists that were organized to resist English taxes
C. Writer of the Declaration of Independence
D. Colonist who wanted to break away from English rule
E. Colonist who remained loyal to the English king
F. Person who raised money to help the colonies fight England
G. Group of colonists that volunteered to fight the English during the Revolutionary War
H. War the colonists fought to become free from England
I. Turning point of the Revolutionary War
J. War fought by the French and English for control of the Ohio Valley
K. Tax on printed materials
L. Document that marked the birth of the United States
M. Document that ruled the former colonies after the Revolutionary War
N. Traitor to the colonist cause
O. One of the rebel leaders
P. Law setting up rules for governing the western lands won from England
Q. Demonstration in which a group of colonists were accidentally killed for protesting English taxes
R. Leader of the colonial army during the Revolutionary War
S. Document that allowed an official to search another person's house without cause
T. Demonstration in which colonists dressed up like Indians and threw English tea into the harbor

7 Heading Toward War

Learning the Vocabulary

Fill in the blank in each of the following sentences with the word that best fits. Use each word in the list below just once.

Patriot	writ of assistance
Stamp Act	Declaration of Independence
smuggling	Loyalist
boycott	Revolutionary War
French and Indian War	Boston Tea Party

1. Between 1754 and 1763, the French and English fought the _____ to gain control of the Ohio Valley.

2. Many colonists refused to pay high English taxes. They started a _____ and refused to buy anything made in England.

3. The _____ put a tax on printed materials such as wills, books, and playing cards.

4. An official could search a person's house without cause with the use of a _____ _____ .

5. When the _____ was signed on July 4, 1776, the United States became an independent country.

6. In the _____ , American colonists dressed up as Indians threw English tea into the harbor to protest English taxes.

7. A _____ was a colonist who wanted the colonies to rule themselves.

8. An American colonist who did not want to break away from English rule was called a _____ _____ .

9. Americans often got around English taxes by illegally buying things made in other countries and sneaking them into the colonies. This is called _____ .

10. American colonists fought the _____ to gain their freedom from England.

8 Taxation Without Representation

Learning the Vocabulary

Unscramble the words in capital letters in each of the sentences below. Write your answers in the blanks at the bottom of the page.

1. The **SNSO FO TLYREBI** were groups of colonists that were organized to resist English taxes.

2. Several American colonists were accidentally killed for protesting English taxes at the **TNOOSB AMRESSCA**.

3. **RANMECMISLIT** was a plan to keep England rich by forcing Americans to trade only with English merchants.

4. Many American colonists became angry about the English taxes and started a **COYTTOB** by refusing to buy anything from England.

5. An American colonist who wanted to break away from English rule was called a **LEBER**.

6. Many colonists refused to follow the English trade laws and turned to **LINGGGMUS** to avoid paying English taxes.

7. The **PAMST TAC** put a tax on all printed materials.

8. During the **TOSBON EAT TARPY**, colonists dressed up as Indians and threw English tea into the harbor to protest English taxes on tea.

9. The **UTNIMENME** were bands of colonists who volunteered to fight the English during the Revolutionary War.

10. Search warrants known as **TRISW FO SANCESIAST** were used by the English to look for goods smuggled in by the colonists.

1. _____

2. _____

3. _____

4. _____

5. _____

6. _____

7. _____

8. _____

9. _____

10. _____

9 Finding the Terms

Learning the Vocabulary

The following words have been used in the main idea section. See if you can find these words in the word search puzzle below. Circle the words. They may be found vertically or horizontally. They may also overlap.

rebels

Stamp Act

French and Indian War

writ of assistance

independence

Revolutionary War

Samuel Adams

minutemen

Boston Tea Party

Sons of Liberty

Boston Massacre

George Washington

Thomas Jefferson

Benedict Arnold

Haym Salomon

Loyalists

```
F  R  E  N  C  H  A  N  D  I  N  D  I  A  N  W  A  R  G
B  T  F  X  D  A  P  C  R  E  B  E  L  S  T  R  D  E  E
V  H  S  C  X  Y  X  X  O  X  F  C  A  C  B  I  R  V  O
S  O  M  W  Z  M  Z  A  B  C  O  X  L  F  O  T  O  O  R
O  M  I  C  I  S  Q  S  O  F  P  C  M  S  S  O  V  L  G
N  A  N  B  N  A  R  T  S  P  L  B  N  A  T  F  W  U  E
S  S  U  L  D  L  J  A  T  Q  Q  A  Q  M  O  A  X  T  W
O  J  T  O  E  O  C  M  O  C  M  F  L  U  N  S  C  I  A
F  E  E  Z  P  M  D  P  N  K  L  I  O  E  M  S  P  O  S
L  F  M  I  E  O  I  A  T  X  U  F  Y  L  A  I  Q  N  H
I  F  E  L  N  T  C  E  O  T  G  A  A  S  S  R  A  I
B  E  N  E  D  I  C  T  A  R  N  O  L  D  S  T  S  R  N
E  R  O  H  E  T  L  F  P  M  V  N  I  A  A  A  B  Y  G
R  S  Q  T  N  X  D  D  A  P  C  I  S  M  C  N  A  W  T
T  O  R  O  C  V  M  L  R  Q  X  N  T  S  R  C  C  A  O
Y  N  X  T  E  O  F  O  T  D  Z  D  S  L  E  E  D  R  N
C  L  Z  D  H  T  F  M  Y  F  Q  E  B  Q  V  O  X  C  B
```

10 Western Land Claims, 1780

Reading Maps and Graphs

One of the problems facing the new government in 1780 was the question of what to do with the claims to land in the west held by some of the states. Since some states had claims and others did not, they disagreed over what should be done with the western land. Study the maps below and then answer the questions that follow.

Western Land Claims, 1780

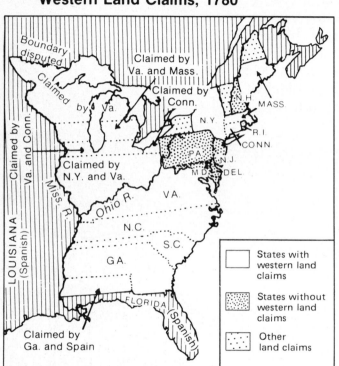

United States Today

1. How many states had western claims? List them. _____

_____

2. Which state had the largest claim on land to the west? _____

3. The Northwest Territory was the land northwest of the Ohio River. Name the four states that had

claims in the Northwest Territory. _____

4. What five present-day states were formed from the Northwest Territory? _____

_____

5. Which original state claimed the area that is now the state of Tennessee? _____

6. List the six original states that had no western land claims. _____

_____

11 The United States, 1783

Reading Maps and Graphs

The Treaty of Paris of 1783 recognized the independence of the United States and set the boundaries of the new nation. Study the map below and then answer the questions that follow.

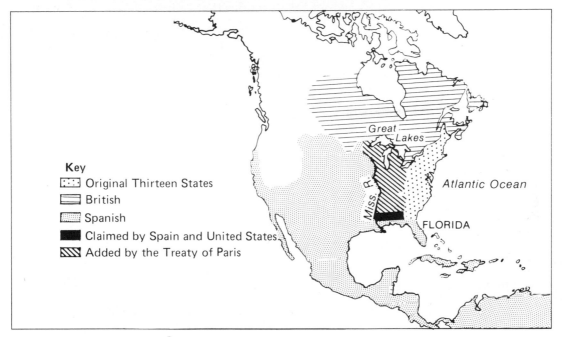

Key
- ⠿ Original Thirteen States
- ▭ British
- ▤ Spanish
- ■ Claimed by Spain and United States
- ▨ Added by the Treaty of Paris

1. How much larger than the thirteen original states was the United States in 1783? _____

_____

2. What was the western boundary of the United States in 1783? _____

3. What was the eastern boundary of the United States? _____

4. What was the northern boundary? _____

5. What was the southern boundary? _____

6. What country claimed Florida? _____

7. What country claimed the land to the west of the United States? _____

8. What country claimed the land to the north of the United States? _____

9. Compare this map with the map of the eastern United States today on page 22. How many

current states are in the area added by the Treaty of Paris of 1783? _____

10. List the states that were added by the Treaty of Paris. _____

_____

12 Land Ordinance of 1785

Reading Maps and Graphs

The Land Ordinance of 1785 established a system for surveying the western land. The land was divided into townships, and these townships were in turn divided into sections. Study the drawings of a typical township and section below. Then answer the questions that follow.

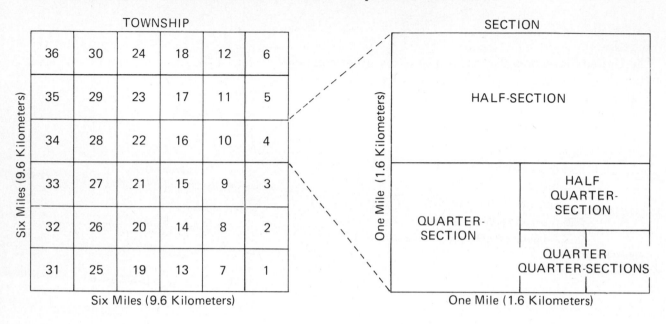

1. Square measures are figured by multiplying the width of an area times its length. How many

square miles are located in each township? _____

2. How many sections are in a township? _____

3. What are the length and width measurements of a section of land? _____

_____

4. A full section contains 640 (256 hectares) acres. How many acres would be in each of the

following? half section _____ , quarter-section _____

_____ , half quarter-section _____ , quarter

quarter-section _____

5. How many quarter-sections are in a section? _____

1   Writing the Constitution

Getting the Main Idea

Read each paragraph below. Then write what you think is the main idea of each paragraph on the lines provided.

1.   The Constitution of the United States was written because government leaders saw the weaknesses of the Articles of Confederation. Under the Articles, the government was too weak to hold the states together. It could not solve many problems facing the new nation. Because of its weak government, the United States was also not respected by other countries. In May 1787, leaders from the different states met at a convention in Philadelphia to rewrite the Articles. They soon found that this would not take care of the country's problems. Instead they wrote the Constitution to set up a whole new form of government.

The main idea of this paragraph is _____

_____

2.   The writers of the Constitution formed a government divided into three separate branches. Each branch would be responsible for a different function. The legislative branch would make the laws. The executive branch would carry out and enforce the laws. The judicial branch would interpret or explain the laws.

The main idea of this paragraph is _____

_____

3.   One of the biggest worries facing the Constitutional Convention was how many representatives each state should have in the legislative branch. The large states favored the Virginia plan. This plan would have states represented on the basis of their population. The small states, led by New Jersey, were afraid this plan would not give them enough voice in government. They came up with their own plan. In the New Jersey plan, each state would have the same number of representatives, no matter what its size. A compromise was finally reached. The two groups agreed that the Congress would be made up of two parts, the Senate and the House of Representatives. In the Senate, each state would have two members. In the House of Representatives, the number of members from each state would depend on that state's population.

The main idea of this paragraph is _____

_____

4.   The Constitution was finished in September 1787. Before it became the law of the land, it had to be ratified, or approved, by nine of the thirteen states. The Federalists were in favor of the Constitution. The Antifederalists thought the new government was too powerful. They wanted a Bill of Rights added to the Constitution. This Bill of Rights would spell out those rights that the government could not take away from the people. These two groups had many disagreements before the Constitution was finally accepted. It was approved by the ninth state in 1788 and by the thirteenth state in 1790.

The main idea of this paragraph is _____

_____

2   Political Problems of the New Nation

Getting the Main Idea

Read each paragraph below. Choose which of the three sentences following each paragraph best states the main idea of that paragraph. Write the letter of that sentence in the blank.

_____ 1.   Secretary of the Treasury Alexander Hamilton and Secretary of State Thomas Jefferson were two of the new country's greatest leaders. But the two men did not agree on any important issue of the day. Hamilton believed that the rich and educated people were best suited to run the country. Jefferson put his faith in the common people. Hamilton favored a strong national government. Jefferson wanted the states to have the greatest power. Hamilton was the leader of the Federalist party. Jefferson led the Republican party. Hamilton thought that a national bank should be set up. Jefferson was against it. Finally, the two men did not agree about how the Constitution should be explained. Hamilton favored a loose, or liberal, interpretation. Jefferson favored a strict, or word-for-word, interpretation.

A.   Hamilton and Jefferson did not agree on most political issues.

B.   Jefferson believed that the national government needed to be made stronger.

C.   Hamilton stood up for the rights of the common people.

_____ 2.   The way of electing the President caused problems in some of the early elections. At that time, the names of all the people running for President and Vice-President were put on the same ballot. The man who received the most electoral votes became President. The man with the second highest number of votes became Vice-President. In 1796, the men who became President and Vice-President were from different parties. Instead of working together, they did not agree at all. In 1800, the Republican candidates for President and Vice-President received the same number of votes. The tie finally had to be broken by the House of Representatives.

A.   Politicians have always tried to confuse the voters.

B.   The elections of 1796 and 1800 were unfair and crooked.

C.   There were problems with the early way of electing the President.

_____ 3.   In 1791, the government placed a tax on whiskey to help pay its debts. Many farmers who turned their extra corn into whiskey thought the tax was unfair. Some refused to pay it. Others beat up tax collectors. This alarmed President George Washington. He sent 15,000 soldiers in to stop the rebellion. The fighting was soon stopped, and the farmers paid their taxes. The Whiskey Rebellion proved that the government could make citizens obey its laws.

A.   The government taxed whiskey to stop people from drinking.

B.   The Whiskey Rebellion proved that the government could enforce its laws.

C.   A person who disagrees with a law does not have to obey it.

_____ 4.   In 1798, the Federalists held the power in Congress. They passed some laws known as the Alien and Sedition Acts. The Federalists used these acts to weaken the Republicans. The Alien Acts gave the President great power. They allowed him to send out of the country any alien he thought dangerous to the safety of the United States. In time of war, the President could jail any person from an enemy country. The Alien Acts also stated that an alien needed to live in the United States for fourteen years before becoming a citizen, instead of for five years as before. Since most aliens joined the Republican party when they became citizens, the Federalists wanted to make it harder for them to become citizens. The Sedition Act set heavy fines and long prison sentences for anyone convicted of finding fault with the government. Several people friendly to Republicans were fined and jailed under this law.

A.   The Alien and Sedition Acts weakened the power of the President.

B.   The Alien and Sedition Acts increased freedom of speech and press.

C.   The Alien and Sedition Acts were used to weaken the Republican party.

3 Relations with Other Nations

Getting the Main Idea

Read each paragraph below. Then underline the sentence that best states the main idea of the paragraph.

1. In 1793, France and England were at war. France expected that the United States would come and fight on its side. After all, France had helped the United States in the Revolutionary War against England. France and the United States had also signed a treaty agreeing to help each other in case of war. President Washington did not want the United States becoming involved in the affairs of other countries. He believed that the United States must remain neutral. Washington thus set forth a Neutrality Proclamation stating that the United States would remain at peace with both France and England.

2. The Barbary pirates of the northern coast of Africa bothered American shipping in that area for many years. These Barbary pirates seized American ships and their cargoes. They also held their crews for ransom. Between 1790 and 1800, the United States paid over $2 million to these pirates. After Thomas Jefferson became President in 1801, they asked for even more money. Jefferson refused. He sent ships into the Mediterranean Sea to fight the pirates. But it was not until 1815 that the United States finally defeated the Barbary pirates and stopped their interference with American shipping.

3. In 1803, France offered to sell its Louisiana Territory to the United States. This large piece of land would more than double the size of the country. The price was also very reasonable. President Jefferson wanted to buy Louisiana. But he was worried about the constitutional problems he thought buying this land would cause. Jefferson was not certain he had the legal power to buy foreign land. He thought an amendment to the Constitution was needed to give him this power. Jefferson's advisers warned him that getting the amendment passed would take too long. They were afraid that the French might change their minds about selling the Louisiana Territory. Seeing that he must act quickly, Jefferson bought Louisiana in spite of his constitutional doubts.

4. John Quincy Adams was one of the United States greatest secretaries of state. In his dealings with other countries, he always tried to protect the peace and freedom of the United States. He also added great amounts of land to the United States. In an 1817 treaty, he was able to reach an agreement with England which limited the number of ships on the Great Lakes. This stopped an arms race between the United States and England. In 1818, he gained the United States greater fishing rights off the coast of Canada. Also in 1818, Adams settled the boundary between the United States and Canada east of the Rocky Mountains. In a treaty with Spain in 1819, he obtained Florida for the United States. The treaty also fixed the southern border of the Louisiana Purchase from the Gulf of Mexico to the Pacific Ocean. Finally in 1823, Adams set forth the basic idea which Monroe put into the Monroe Doctrine.

5. The Monroe Doctrine of 1823 was a strong warning to Europe to keep out of the Western Hemisphere. In a speech before Congress, President James Monroe warned that no parts of North or South America were open to further colonization by European countries. He stated that the United States would think of any European interference with the governments in the Western Hemisphere as an unfriendly act. The Monroe Doctrine also stated that the United States would not interfere in the internal affairs of European countries.

4 The War of 1812

Getting the Main Idea

Read each paragraph below. Choose which of the three sentences following each paragraph best states the main idea of that paragraph. Write the letter of that sentence in the blank.

_____ 1.   The United States went to war with England in 1812 because England refused to treat the United States as a neutral country. England often interfered with American freedom of the seas. The English navy impressed, or kidnapped, men off American ships and forced them to join the English navy. English ships often hindered American fishing off the coast of Newfoundland. English ships also took cargo off American ships headed for France. English interference was not limited to the sea. England still had several forts in the American territory and Canada. Soldiers from these forts encouraged Indians to attack American settlers.

   A. The United States did not respect English rights at sea.

   B. The War of 1812 was caused by English interference in American affairs.

   C. American settlers encouraged Indians to attack English forts in Canada.

_____ 2.   The Battle of New Orleans, the greatest American victory in the War of 1812, was really fought after the war was over. As a result, the battle had no influence on the outcome of the war. The American general Andrew Jackson won a decisive victory over the English at New Orleans. But unknown to Jackson, peace negotiations between England and the Americans had already begun. Indeed, the Treaty of Ghent, ending the War of 1812, was signed in Europe two weeks before the Battle of New Orleans. Since communication was slow in those times, news that the war was over did not reach New Orleans until after the battle.

   A. The Battle of New Orleans was fought after the War of 1812 was over.

   B. England won the Battle of New Orleans.

   C. The Battle of New Orleans decided which nation won the War of 1812.

_____ 3.   The War of 1812 was not very popular in the New England states. People there were upset because the war hurt their businesses. Their businesses depended on trade with Europe, especially England. During the War of 1812, this trade was stopped. The New England states refused to support the war. They refused to loan money to the government to help pay for the costs of the war. They also refused to furnish their share of soldiers to fight the war. In 1814, leaders from the New England states met at the Hartford Convention. They agreed that the war must be stopped. Some leaders even threatened to leave the Union and make a separate peace treaty with England. The war ended, however, before any such action was taken.

   A. The War of 1812 was good for business in New England.

   B. The New England states were against the War of 1812.

   C. The Hartford Convention voted to send more money and troops for the war.

_____ 4.   When the War of 1812 was over, both the United States and England realized that they had gained nothing. None of the major causes of the war were even mentioned in the Treaty of Ghent, which ended the war. The border between Canada and the United States remained where it had been before the war began. The problem of freedom of the sea was not settled. Nothing was said about English impressment of American sailors in the peace treaty. The question of American fishing rights was also omitted. These were the issues which had led to war. But the treaty did not settle them.

   A. The United States won the War of 1812.

   B. The United States gained part of Canada as a result of the War of 1812.

   C. The War of 1812 settled none of the problems which had caused it.

5 After the Revolution

Learning the Vocabulary

Fill in the blank in each of the following sentences with the word that best fits. Use each word in the list below just once.

Constitutional Convention Alexander Hamilton
Whiskey Rebellion election of 1796
Articles of Confederation Thomas Jefferson
Federalist Republican
compromise Louisiana Purchase

1. The ———————— started because many farmers refused to pay a tax on the whiskey they made.

2. The ———————— party supported the adoption of the Constitution and wanted a strong national government.

3. The United States concluded the ———————— with France in 1803.

4. ———————— was secretary of the treasury under President George Washington and the leader of the Federalist party.

5. The ———————— was unusual because the President and the Vice-President were elected from two different political parties.

6. The ———————— was the first plan of government for the United States immediately following the Revolutionary War.

7. The ———————— was the meeting where the Constitution of the United States was written.

8. ———————— was the President of the United States during the Louisiana Purchase.

9. The Alien and Sedition Acts were used to weaken the ———————— party.

10. A ———————— is a settlement of a dispute worked out by both sides giving in on certain points.

6 Constitution

Learning the Vocabulary

Unscramble the words in capital letters in each of the sentences below. Write your answers in the blanks at the bottom of the page.

1. The number of members each state has in the **UOHES FO PERSERTNEITASEV** is decided by its population.

2. Each state has two **ANOTESSR** to represent them in Congress.

3. The Senate and House of Representatives are in the **ALISGELVITE** branch of the government.

4. The **DUCILAIJ** branch of government is responsible for interpreting the laws of the country.

5. Alexander Hamilton favored a **EOSOL** interpretation of the Constitution. According to this interpretation, the meaning of the Constitution can be "bent" to include ideas not actually stated.

6. The **NIOTUTALTISOCN NOCNEVOITN** was a meeting of delegates from various states that drew up a new plan of government.

7. The **WNE YSEEJR LPNA** was a suggestion that the smaller states have a larger voice in the federal government.

8. The **INTADREATSSILFE** were a group that opposed the ratification of the Constitution because it gave too much power to the central government.

9. The **ISNOTCUTITON** is a document laying down the rules for running the government.

10. The **GVAIINIR ALPN** was a suggestion that the larger states have a much larger voice in the federal government.

1. _____   6. _____

2. _____   7. _____

3. _____   8. _____

4. _____   9. _____

5. _____   10. _____

7 Before and During the War of 1812

Learning the Vocabulary

Read each sentence below. Then complete the sentence by filling in the spaces correctly. Each dash represents one letter in the correct spelling of the word.

1. The _ _ _ _ _ _   _ _ _ _ _ _ _ were a group of men from the northern coast of

    Africa who seized American ships.

2. The _ _ _   _ _   _ _ _ _ was caused by English interference in American affairs. It

    is sometimes called the second Revolutionary War.

3. The _ _ _ _ _ _ _ _ _ _ of sailors was the practice of kidnapping American sailors

    These men were forced to serve on English warships.

4. The _ _ _ _ _ _ _   _ _ _ _ _ _ _ _ _ _ was a meeting of New England statesmen

    opposed to the War of 1812.

5. The _ _ _ _   _ _ _   _ _ _ _ _ _ _ _   _ _ _ _ were laws that were used to arrest

    people who disagreed with the federal government.

6. The _ _ _ _ _ _   _ _   _ _ _   _ _ _ _ _ _ _ was fought after the War of 1812 was

    actually over.

7. The _ _ _ _ _ _   _ _   _ _ _ _ _ was the agreement between England and the United

    States that ended the War of 1812.

8. The _ _ _ _ _ _   _ _ _ _ _ _ _ _ _ warned European countries not to interfere in affairs

    in the Western Hemisphere.

9. Washington's _ _ _ _ _ _ _ _ _   _ _ _ _ _ _ _ _ _ _ _ _ _ stated that the United

    States would remain neutral about other countries' problems.

10. In the election of 1800, the candidates for President and Vice-President received the same

    number of electoral votes. The election was decided by the   _ _ _ _ _   _ _

    _ _ _ _ _ _ _ _ _ _ _ _ _ _ _ _ _.

8 The Early Years

Learning the Vocabulary

Fill in the squares to spell out the names or terms described in the clues.

ACROSS

3. Settlement of a dispute by each side giving a little
6. First President of the United States
7. Two members sent to Congress from each state
8. President of the United States at the time of Louisiana Purchase
9. Political party headed by Alexander Hamilton
10. Kidnapping of American sailors by the English navy

DOWN

1. One of the United States greatest secretaries of state
2. Branch of government made up of the House of Representatives and the Senate
4. Addition to the Constitution demanded by the Antifederalists
5. City where the greatest battle of the War of 1812 was fought after the war was actually over

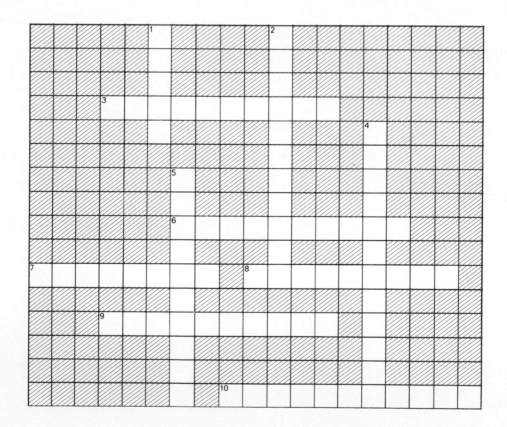

9   The New Government

Learning the Vocabulary

The following words have been used in the main idea section. See if you can find these words in the word search puzzle below. Circle the words. The words may be found vertically or horizontally. They may also overlap.

Constitution
senators
legislative
executive
loose
strict
Barbary pirates
impressment

compromise
Whiskey Rebellion
Federalist
Jefferson
Louisiana Purchase
Monroe
Hamilton
Virginia plan

```
W  H  I  S  K  E  Y  R  E  B  E  L  L  I  O  N  V
B  A  R  B  A  R  Y  P  I  R  A  T  E  S  C  C  I
T  M  S  L  C  T  T  K  M  C  W  C  X  C  O  F  R
C  I  G  E  X  S  C  E  P  E  S  D  E  D  M  S  G
W  L  V  G  U  E  D  C  R  D  T  A  C  O  P  C  I
X  T  O  I  M  N  P  D  E  P  C  T  U  F  R  T  N
L  O  O  S  E  A  B  P  S  A  S  F  T  D  O  I  I
M  N  C  L  R  T  O  Q  S  B  T  R  I  T  M  D  A
O  C  T  A  S  O  F  Z  M  L  R  C  V  L  I  N  P
N  V  B  T  Q  R  L  W  E  O  I  X  E  O  S  B  L
R  X  A  I  X  S  M  C  N  N  C  Q  N  M  E  O  A
O  C  C  V  C  O  N  S  T  I  T  U  T  I  O  N  N
E  X  F  E  D  E  R  A  L  I  S  T  C  X  V  T  C
L  O  U  I  S  I  A  N  A  P  U  R  C  H  A  S  E
J  E  F  F  E  R  S  O  N  T  V  Q  Z  W  A  B  D
```

10 Ratification of the Constitution

Reading Maps and Graphs

Study the chart below and then answer the questions that follow.

State	Date of Ratification	Vote (For and Against)	Order of Ratification
Connecticut	January 9, 1788	128–40	
Delaware	December 7, 1787	Unanimous	
Georgia	January 2, 1788	Unanimous	
Massachusetts	February 6, 1788	187–168	
Maryland	April 28, 1788	63–11	
North Carolina	November 21, 1789	194–77	
New Hampshire	June 21, 1788	57–47	
New Jersey	December 18, 1787	Unanimous	
New York	July 26, 1788	30–27	
Pennsylvania	December 12, 1787	46–23	
Rhode Island	May 29, 1790	34–32	
South Carolina	May 23, 1788	149–73	
Virginia	June 25, 1788	89–79	

1. In the column at the far right, number the states (1, 2, 3, and so on) in the order in which they ratified the Constitution.

2. Which was the first state to ratify the Constitution? _____

3. Which was the last state to ratify the Constitution? _____

4. Nine states were needed to assure the adoption of the Constitution. Which was the ninth state to ratify the Constitution? _____

5. In which states was ratification unanimous? _____

6. In which four states was the ratification vote closest? _____

_____

7. Which state ratified the Constitution by the largest number of votes? _____

11   The United States, 1819

Reading Maps and Graphs

After the new nation was organized, people began to move into the western territories that belonged to the United States. As a result, several new states were added to the nation in the next thirty years. The map below shows the original thirteen states and the new states that were added by 1819. Study the map and then answer the questions that follow.

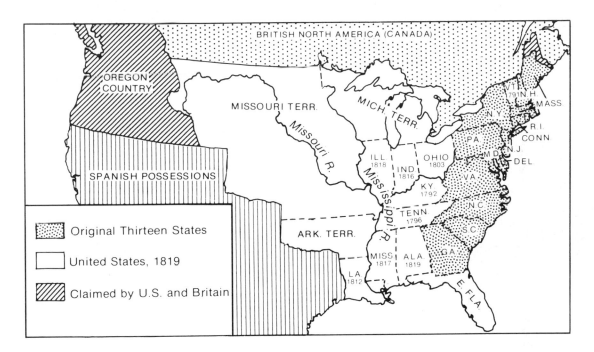

1. How many new states were added by 1819? _____

2. List the new states in the order in which they were added to the Union between 1791 and 1819.

    _____

    _____

3. In which direction were most of the new states in relation to the original thirteen states? _____

4. Which new state is not in the same general location with the rest of the new states? _____

5. What territories were part of the United States in 1819? _____

    _____

12 United States Population, 1790–1830

Reading Maps and Graphs

Study the graph below and then answer the questions that follow.

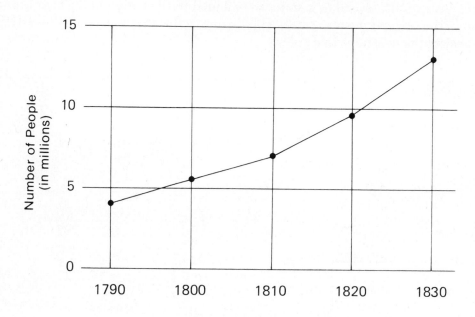

1. Did the population of the United States increase or decrease between 1790 and 1830? _____

2. What was the approximate increase in population between the following years?

A. 1790–1800 _____

B. 1800–1810 _____

C. 1810–1820 _____

D. 1820–1830 _____

3. Which ten-year period experienced the biggest growth in population? _____

4. Which ten-year period showed the least growth in population? _____

5. Approximately how much did the population increase during this forty-year period? _____

1 Age of Jackson

Getting the Main Idea

Read each paragraph below. Then write what you think is the main idea of each paragraph on the lines provided.

1. In 1824, four men ran for President—John Quincy Adams, William Crawford, Henry Clay, and Andrew Jackson. Jackson won more popular and electoral votes than the other three men. But he did not have the majority of 131 electoral votes needed to become President. In such a case, the House of Representatives had to pick the President from the top three men. Since Clay had received the fewest votes, he was out of the running. Clay threw his support to Adams. Clay's influence in the House was great enough to assure Adams' election. Soon after the election, President Adams made Clay his secretary of state. An angry Andrew Jackson charged that Clay and Adams had made a "corrupt bargain" to rob him of the presidency.

The main idea of this paragraph is _____

_____

2. In 1829, Andrew Jackson took office as President after running again. Jackson was different from all the Presidents before him. All the others had come from wealthy backgrounds and were highly educated. Jackson had been born in a log cabin and had no formal education. All the other Presidents had come from Massachusetts or Virginia. Jackson was the first President from a western state, Tennessee. Most important, Jackson had a different view of his office. The other Presidents had thought their job was just to carry out the laws made by Congress. Jackson had little respect for Congress. He often acted as he thought the people would wish him to act.

The main idea of this paragraph is _____

_____

3. Andrew Jackson believed that the common people should have a chance to hold public office. He thought it was unfair that only rich and educated people had government jobs. When Jackson became President, he fired many government officials and put his own friends and supporters in their place. This became known as the spoils system. The name came from the old saying "To the victors belong the spoils."

The main idea of this paragraph is _____

_____

4. An old Indian fighter, President Jackson believed that the Indians blocked settlement by the whites. Jackson wanted all Indians living east of the Mississippi River to give up their lands to white settlers. The Indians would then be settled in reservations west of the Mississippi. The Cherokees did not want to leave their home in Georgia. The Supreme Court upheld their right to remain there. But since the Supreme Court had no power to enforce its ruling, Jackson ignored it. He ordered the army to move the Cherokees to Oklahoma. Nearly one-quarter of the Indians died along the march, which became known as the Trail of Tears.

The main idea of this paragraph is _____

_____

2 Expansion

Getting the Main Idea

Read each paragraph below. Then underline the sentence that best states the main idea of each paragraph.

1. When the United States bought the Louisiana Territory from France in 1803, not much was known about the area. The exact boundaries were not clear. No one knew what would be found there. In 1804, Captain Meriwether Lewis and Lieutenant William Clark were sent out to explore the Louisiana Territory. When they returned two years later, Lewis and Clark gave the country valuable information about the Louisiana Territory. They described in great detail the plants and animals found there. They brought back soil and rock samples. Lewis and Clark learned much about the Indians living there. They also suggested routes for later settlers. Their journals proved very useful to mapmakers.

2. Before the National Road was built, rough wilderness trails were the only form of overland transportation connecting the different parts of the United States. Western farmers found it nearly impossible to send their crops to the eastern cities. Eastern factories were also unable to ship their goods to the western settlements. In 1811, the Congress acted on these problems. The National Road, also known as the Cumberland Road, was built to link the East and the Northwest Territory, the land northwest of the Ohio River. By 1838, it ran from Maryland as far west as Illinois. The National Road became the major route for trade between the East and West.

3. Finished in 1825, the Erie Canal connected Lake Erie and the Hudson River in New York. The Erie Canal greatly reduced shipping costs and provided transportation for settlers moving to the Midwest. Before the canal was built, it cost one hundred dollars to ship a ton of cargo between Buffalo and New York City. After the canal was built, the shipping cost dropped to only five dollars per ton. Because the canal made it cheaper and easier for farmers to ship their crops, the value of crops grown in the Ohio Valley doubled. Besides making shipping costs lower, the Erie Canal provided easy and inexpensive transportation to farmers eager to settle in the Midwest. Pioneers found that travel on the canal was easier than overland. To many, the Erie Canal was the best route west.

4. In the 1830s, many Americans were drawn to the Oregon Territory, the land west of the Louisiana Purchase. The climate there was excellent. The country had many natural resources such as furs, lumber, and fish. Sailing from harbors on the Oregon coast, ships carried on trade with Asia. They sailed with goods sent overland from the eastern states and returned with goods from across the Pacific. Christian missionaries wanted to convert the Indians in the Oregon Territory. National pride was also involved. Oregon was claimed by both the United States and England. Many Americans went to Oregon to make the United States claim there stronger.

5. The United States gained much Mexican land as a result of the Mexican War. The Mexican War began in 1846 over a disagreement with Mexico about the southern border of Texas. But the United States was also eager for a war with Mexico as an excuse to expand into Mexican territory. The war ended in 1848 with the signing of the Treaty of Guadalupe Hidalgo. According to the terms of this treaty, the United States won the land it was after. Mexico was forced to cede, or give up, almost two-fifths of its land. The land the United States gained was known as the Mexican Cession. It was almost as large as the Louisiana Purchase. It included all of what now are the states of New Mexico, Arizona, California, and Utah, as well as parts of Colorado and Wyoming.

3 Who Should Have Power?

Getting the Main Idea

Read each paragraph below. Choose which of the three sentences following each paragraph best states the main idea of that paragraph. Write the letter of that sentence in the blank.

_____ 1. John Marshall helped strengthen the power of the national government. Marshall was chief justice of the Supreme Court from 1801 until 1835. During those years, he ruled on hundreds of cases. Marshall believed that the Constitution gave greater power to the federal government than to the states. In one case, he ruled that a state government could not ignore the ruling of a federal court. By doing this, he gave national courts authority over the state courts. In another case, Marshall said that states could not interfere with the power of Congress to control trade between states.
   A. John Marshall wanted to increase the power of the state governments.
   B. John Marshall worked to strengthen the power of national government.
   C. John Marshall preferred state courts over federal courts.

_____ 2. By 1800, there were important differences between the various sections of the United States. The Northeast was strong in industry and trade. The South had become a land of cotton plantations run by slaves. The Northwest, settled by pioneers, was a land of small farms. Americans all over the country became torn between their loyalty for their own section and their loyalty to their country as a whole. Instead of working together to find answers to the country's problems, Americans were worried about the interests of their own section. This is known as sectionalism.
   A. Sectionalism means people care more about their own section than about the country.
   B. Sectionalism means that the Northwest was the fastest growing section.
   C. There are few differences between the different sections of the country.

_____ 3. By 1830, the North and the South were disagreeing strongly over whether the states or the national government should be more powerful. The Hayne-Webster debate took place in the Senate over this question. Robert Hayne, a southern senator, thought that the states should have the most power. He believed that the states should decide which laws they would or would not obey. This would keep the national government from having too much power. A northern senator named Daniel Webster did not agree. He defended the power of the national government. He stated that it was the people from the whole country, not just the states, who made up the Union.
   A. Webster wanted the states to have more power.
   B. Hayne wanted the national government to be more powerful.
   C. The Hayne-Webster debate shows the disagreement over whether the states or the national government should be more powerful.

_____ 4. In 1819, Missouri asked to become a state. This caused several problems. At that time, there were the same number of slave states as free states. If Missouri became a slave state as it asked, this balance would be upset. Since Missouri would be the first state to enter from the Louisiana Territory, it would set a pattern for other states to follow. Congress carefully settled these problems by passing the Missouri Compromise of 1820. Missouri was admitted as a slave state, while Maine was added as a free state. To settle future questions about slavery, a line was drawn west from the southern border of Missouri. Above this line would be free states. Below this line would be slave states. In this way, the Missouri Compromise kept the balance between slave states and free states.
   A. Slavery was forbidden in all of the Louisiana Purchase.
   B. Missouri wanted to become the first free state in the South.
   C. The Missouri Compromise kept the balance between free and slave states.

4 Economic Disagreements

Getting the Main Idea

Read each paragraph below. Choose which of the three sentences following each paragraph best states the main idea of that paragraph. Write the letter of that sentence in the blank.

_____ 1. In 1816, John Calhoun of South Carolina introduced in Congress a bill calling for the government to set aside $1,500,000 to pay for improvements such as the building of roads and canals. Many people did not like Calhoun's Bonus Bill because it ran against their sectional interests. People in New England already had good roads. They were against the bill. They did not want government money spent on other sections. The Bonus Bill barely passed Congress in 1817. But President James Madison vetoed the bill the day before he left office.
  A. Calhoun's Bonus Bill faced much opposition because of sectionalism.
  B. President Madison gladly signed the Bonus Bill into law.
  C. New England strongly supported Calhoun's Bonus Bill.

_____ 2. A new tariff, a tax on imported goods, was passed by the United States government in 1828. This tariff was very unpopular in the South, particularly in South Carolina. Southern leaders believed that the tariff helped protect only northern factories. They said it raised the price of goods that the South bought from other countries. A special meeting held in South Carolina passed a nullification ordinance. This act stated that the tariff was not constitutional. It also said that the people did not have to pay the tax. If the government tried to make people pay it, South Carolina threatened to leave the Union.
  A. South Carolina thought the nullification ordinance was unconstitutional.
  B. The northern states opposed the tariff of 1828.
  C. South Carolina was angry about the tariff of 1828.

_____ 3. President Jackson did not like the national bank. The bank was really a group of banks set up by the government as a safe place to store its money. The bank was also intended to make it easier for people and businesses to borrow money. But Jackson believed that the bank was harming the country. He thought that it helped only the rich bankers and business leaders in the East. The charter that had formed the bank ran out in 1836. In order for the bank to go on operating, the President had to sign a bill to recharter it. But Jackson vetoed the bill. He also removed the government's money from the national bank and put it into several state banks.
  A. President Jackson opposed the national bank.
  B. The common people made large fortunes by investing in the national bank.
  C. President Jackson created the national bank in 1836.

_____ 4. In 1837, the United States entered a bad depression known as the panic of 1837. President Jackson's Specie Circular of 1836 was a major cause of this depression. Jackson had been worried that too much paper money had been issued during the sale of western land to the public. So Jackson put forth the Specie Circular. It ordered the government to accept only gold or silver coins, known as specie, as payment for the sale of public land. In other words, the government would no longer accept paper money. Land prices fell because most people did not have the gold or silver to buy land. People asked their banks to exchange their paper money for specie. By 1837, many banks had run out of gold and silver and were forced to close. Workers became unemployed as the factories closed and construction on railroads and canals stopped.
  A. President Jackson forced the banks to accept only paper money.
  B. Jackson's Specie Circular was a major cause of the panic of 1837.
  C. The Specie Circular caused the price of western land to increase.

5 The Jackson Years

Learning the Vocabulary

Fill in the blank in each of the following sentences with the word that best fits. Use each word in the list below just once.

Andrew Jackson	nullification ordinance
corrupt bargain	John Quincy Adams
tariff	Specie Circular
spoils system	panic of 1837
Trail of Tears	national bank

1. The _____ was a group of banks set up by the federal government.

   President Jackson opposed this concept. He vetoed a bill to recharter these banks.

2. A _____ is a tax applied to imported goods.

3. The _____ passed by South Carolina stated that the federal tariff

   of 1828 was unconstitutional.

4. _____ , who served as President of the United States from 1829 to

   1837, was the first President from a western state.

5. Under the _____ , politicians who have won an election give their

   followers jobs held by members of the party that has lost.

6. The _____ required the people of the United States to pay for

   government land with only gold or silver.

7. The _____ was a depression that happened after President Jackson

   issued the Specie Circular.

8. The _____ was the forced march of the Cherokees from their

   original home in Georgia to a reservation in Oklahoma.

9. The election of 1824 was decided by the House of Representatives. Henry Clay's support enabled

   _____ to become the President.

10. Angered by not winning the 1824 election, Andrew Jackson charged Clay and the new President

    with having made a _____ .

6 Nationalism and Expansion

Learning the Vocabulary

Unscramble the words in capital letters in each of the sentences below. Write your answers in the blanks at the bottom of the page.

1. The **IEER AANCL,** which was completed in 1825, has often been called the "big ditch." The "big ditch" connected the Hudson River and Lake Erie in the state of New York.

2. **NHJO RAHSMALL** was a chief justice of the United States Supreme Court from 1801 until 1835. A loyal Federalist, he favored a strong federal government.

3. The **NOROGE RTIRETRYO** was the land west of the Louisiana Purchase which was claimed by both the United States and England.

4. The **YENHA-BTSREEW BEAETD** was a disagreement in the United States Senate over whether the states or the national government should be the most powerful.

5. In 1804, Captain Meriwether **IWESL** and Lieutenant William **RKCAL** were chosen to explore the new Louisiana Territory west of the Mississippi River.

6. The **LNANAIOT ADRO** ran from northern Maryland across the Appalachian Mountains to Illinois.

7. The **IXNACEM SESNIOC** was the land the United States gained as the result of its war with Mexico.

8. Through the **USOSIMRI MRPOCIMOES,** Missouri was admitted to the United States as a slave state and Maine as a free state.

9. **ETLAMISSCINO** means that people are more concerned about the interests of their own area than with the good of the entire country.

10. The **SUONB LILB** was a proposal by John Calhoun that government pay for the cost of building roads, canals, and other public works.

1. _____   6. _____

2. _____   7. _____

3. _____   8. _____

4. _____   9. _____

5. _____   10. _____

7 Filling in the Puzzle

Learning the Vocabulary

Fill in the squares to spell out the names or terms described in the clues.

ACROSS

1. Law admitting Missouri as a slave state and Maine as a free state
6. Group of banks chartered by the federal government
9. Border disagreement settled by the Treaty of Guadalupe Hidalgo
10. Tax on imported goods

DOWN

2. Political practice of putting one's friends into political jobs
3. Land west of the Louisiana Purchase claimed by the United States and Britain
4. Chief justice of the United States who favored a strong national government
5. The "big ditch" connecting the Hudson River and Lake Erie
7. Calhoun's suggestion that the federal government pay for the cost of internal improvements such as roads and canals
8. Two leaders of the expedition that explored the Louisiana Purchase

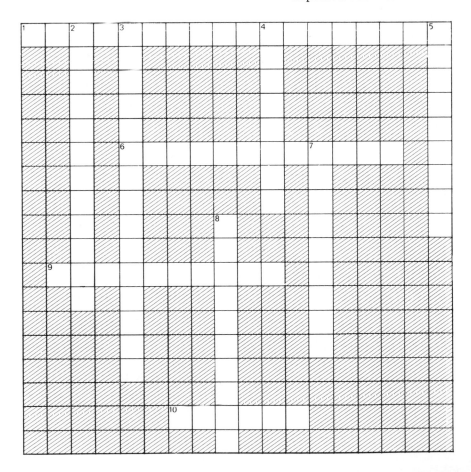

8 The Nation

Learning the Vocabulary

The following words have been used in the main idea section. See if you can find these words in the word search puzzle below. Circle the words. They may be found vertically or horizontally. They may also overlap.

Erie Canal	Bonus Bill
Marshall	national bank
Oregon Territory	Clay
Lewis and Clark	nullification
National Road	Jackson
Mexican War	tariff
Trail of Tears	spoils system
sectionalism	Adams

```
E   R   T   R   A   I   L   O   F   T   E   A   R   S   N   G

R   M   Z   S   N   W   P   R   P   C   B   A   J   A   A   L

I   E   B   E   A   E   C   E   Q   B   L   D   A   L   T   E

E   X   N   C   T   C   E   G   A   O   D   A   C   O   I   W

C   I   L   T   I   G   D   O   C   T   Q   M   K   C   O   I

A   C   M   I   O   M   O   N   S   L   E   S   S   B   N   S

N   A   C   O   N   P   X   T   W   C   S   L   O   D   A   A

A   N   H   N   A   T   C   E   X   B   C   O   N   H   L   N

L   W   I   A   L   S   A   R   B   C   L   P   A   U   R   D

D   A   L   L   B   M   A   R   S   H   A   L   L   L   O   C

G   R   O   I   A   V   T   I   A   I   Y   D   T   M   A   L

L   C   P   S   N   A   O   T   A   R   I   F   F   P   D   A

D   T   R   M   K   C   B   O   N   U   S   B   I   L   L   R

Q   U   T   Z   C   D   O   R   C   C   A   C   P   Z   V   K

S   P   O   I   L   S   S   Y   S   T   E   M   Q   S   W   U

N   U   L   L   I   F   I   C   A   T   I   O   N   Z   F   B
```

9   The National Road

Reading Maps and Graphs

As you have read, the National Road became a major route between the East and the West. Study the map of the National Road below and then answer the questions that follow.

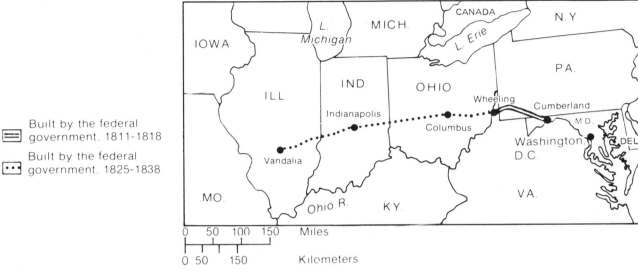

Built by the federal
government. 1811-1818

Built by the federal
government. 1825-1838

1. In what general direction did the National Road run? _____

2. Where did the National Road begin? _____

3. What town was at the end of the National Road in 1818? _____

_____

4. In 1818, how many miles (kilometers) long was the National Road? _____

_____

5. What town marked the end of the National Road in 1838? _____

6. How long was the National Road in 1838? _____

7. By 1838, what three present-day states were opened up to greater settlement by the National

Road? _____

8. What river near the National Road provided transportation in the same general direction? _____

_____

10 Exploration of the West

Reading Maps and Graphs

Exploration of the West early in the nineteenth century opened up this land to settlement later in the century. Study the map about Lewis and Clark's and Pike's expeditions. Then answer the questions that follow.

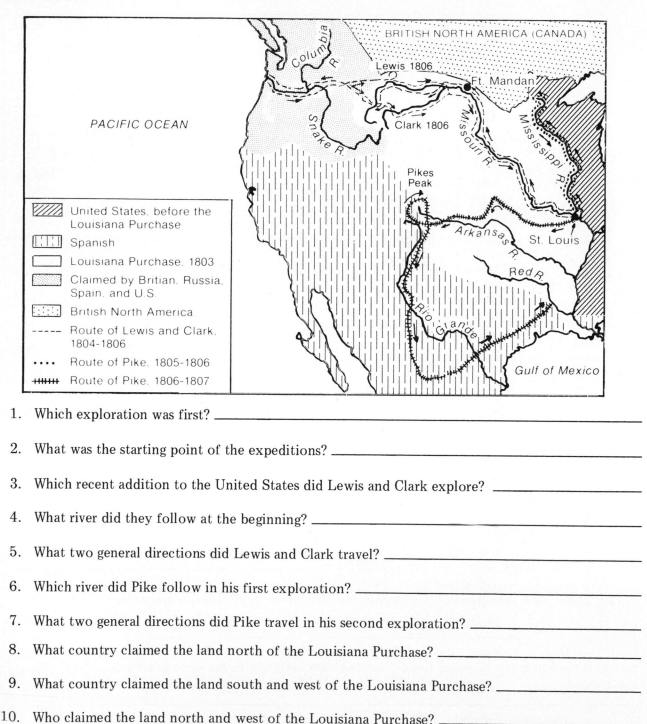

1. Which exploration was first? _____

2. What was the starting point of the expeditions? _____

3. Which recent addition to the United States did Lewis and Clark explore? _____

4. What river did they follow at the beginning? _____

5. What two general directions did Lewis and Clark travel? _____

6. Which river did Pike follow in his first exploration? _____

7. What two general directions did Pike travel in his second exploration? _____

8. What country claimed the land north of the Louisiana Purchase? _____

9. What country claimed the land south and west of the Louisiana Purchase? _____

10. Who claimed the land north and west of the Louisiana Purchase? _____

11 Missouri Compromise of 1820

Reading Maps and Graphs

The Missouri Compromise of 1820 kept the balance between slave and free states. It also temporarily settled the dispute over slavery in the territories. Study the map below and then answer the questions that follow.

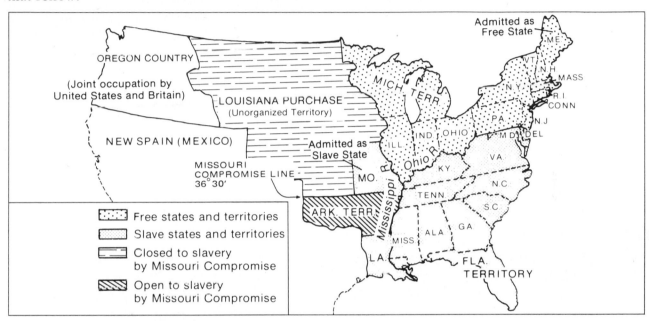

1. Under the terms of the Missouri Compromise, two states were admitted to the Union. What

state was admitted as a free state? _____

2. What state was admitted as a slave state? _____

3. After these two states were admitted, how many slave states were there? _____

4. How many free states were there after the Missouri Compromise? _____

5. What territory was free before 1820? _____

6. In what territory was slavery allowed before 1820? _____

7. What territory was closed to slavery by the Missouri Compromise? _____

8. What territory was opened to slavery by the Missouri Compromise? _____

9. According to the Missouri Compromise, what divided the area open to slavery from the area

closed to slavery? _____

10. What area was occupied by both the United States and Britain? _____

12   Expansion of the United States

Reading Maps and Graphs

By 1853, the United States had acquired all the land that made up the first forty-eight states. Study the map below and then answer the questions that follow.

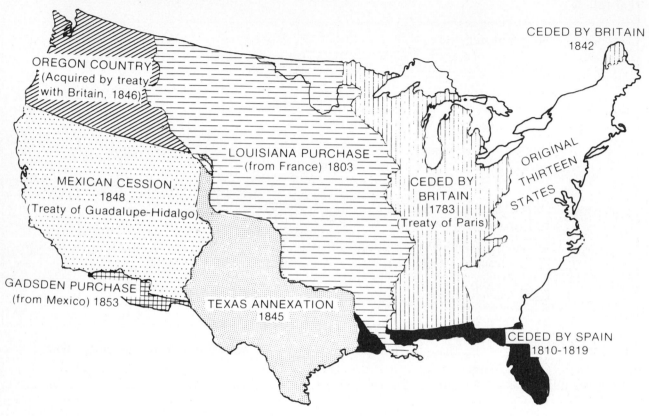

1. From which country did the United States acquire the following territories?

A. Louisiana Purchase _____   D. Gadsden Purchase _____

B. Oregon country _____   E. Florida _____

C. Mexican Cession _____

2. How did the United States acquire Texas? _____

3. Which direction were most of these territories in relation to the original thirteen states? _____

_____

4. What territory lay to the south of the original thirteen states? _____

5. Which territory added the most land to the United States? _____

6. Which territory added the smallest amount of land to the United States? _____

_____

1 Slavery

Getting the Main Idea

Read each paragraph below. Then write what you think is the main idea of each paragraph on the lines provided.

1. The Atlantic crossing was a terrible voyage for Africans being shipped to the New World. After the Africans had been captured and sold into slavery, they were herded onto the ships like cattle. They were generally chained together below deck. The heat was often unbearable. The slaves had little food and little chance to move about. Some of the slaves tried to kill themselves by jumping into the sea rather than face such terrible conditions. Others refused to eat and starved to death. Sometimes the slaves would try to revolt against the crew to win their freedom. Their revolts generally failed, and those who took part were killed. Sharks sometimes followed the ships, waiting for the dead to be thrown into the ocean.

The main idea of this paragraph is _____

_____

2. In 1808, Congress passed a law making it illegal for more slaves to be brought into the country. Both slave traders and slave owners ignored this law. Traders smuggled slaves into the country. They had no trouble finding buyers. The cotton gin, invented by Eli Whitney, had made it possible for southern planters to grow more cotton. This machine could separate seeds from cotton fifty times faster than could be done by hand. More slaves were needed to grow and harvest the larger crops. Between 1808 and 1860, about 300,000 slaves were smuggled into the South.

The main idea of this paragraph is _____

_____

3. All slaves in the United States were not treated the same. Their treatment depended on such things as the personality of the master, the size of the plantation, and their own age, sex, and health. Household slaves and skilled workers were generally treated well. But most slaves worked in the fields. They faced long hours of backbreaking work. They were often poorly fed, housed, and clothed. If they did not obey orders, they were beaten.

The main idea of this paragraph is _____

_____

4. In the middle of the 1800s, a group of southern writers began to defend slavery. In their view, blacks were too backward to care for themselves. Therefore, blacks were better off than they were before they became slaves. They received food, clothing, and housing. The sick and aged were cared for. Compared to slaves, northern factory workers were not treated as well. Slavery, it was said, benefited the whole South. It provided free labor. It also prevented strikes. Some writers even thought that other workers, black and white, in both the North and South, should be slaves as well. The best-known of these defenders of slavery was George Fitzhugh.

The main idea of this paragraph is _____

_____

2   Abolitionists

Getting the Main Idea

Read each paragraph below. Then underline the sentence that best states the main idea of each paragraph.

1.   Abolitionists were people who wanted to abolish, or end, slavery. They believed that one person should not be allowed to own another. In their view, slavery went against the Bible. They also believed it was against the American ideal that all people are equal. Abolitionists worked hard to convince others that slaves must be freed. A well-known speaker at abolitionist meetings was Frederick Douglass, an escaped slave. He described the horrors of slavery to people all over the North. Another leader was William Lloyd Garrison. Garrison published *The Liberator,* a powerful abolitionist newspaper. Other abolitionists helped runaway slaves escape from their masters. A few even raised money to buy a slave's freedom.

2.   The American Colonization Society was formed to free slaves and send them to Africa. The Society set up the colony of Liberia (meaning "freedom") in Africa for freed slaves. For several reasons, the Society was not very successful. The chief reason was the growing cost of slaves. A slave could cost as much as two thousand dollars. The Society could buy only a few blacks to ship back to Africa. Another reason why the Society failed was that free blacks did not want to go to Africa. Their families had lived in the United States for several generations. To these blacks, Africa was a strange and far-off land. Between 1816 and 1831, the Society sent less than 1,500 people to Liberia.

3.   The underground railroad was a system to help slaves escape from their masters. Volunteers known as "conductors" led slaves to freedom in the North or in British North America (Canada). They traveled at night so that slave hunters would not see them. During the day, they rested in secret hiding places, such as attics or haylofts. These were known as "stations." Harriet Tubman, herself an escaped slave, was the most famous conductor on the underground railroad. She made nineteen trips to the South and led about three hundred slaves to freedom.

4.   Harriet Beecher Stowe's book *Uncle Tom's Cabin* was one of the most widely read and influential works of fiction ever written in the United States. Published in 1852, it sold over 300,000 copies in less than a year. A strong abolitionist, Harriet Beecher Stowe wanted to show how slavery brutalized both owners and slaves. The book is filled with highly emotional scenes picturing the evils of slavery. Southern readers protested that the book falsely showed them as cruel masters. Northern readers were outraged by the treatment of slaves described. Many northern readers were won over to the abolitionist side. The book's effect was so great that when President Lincoln greeted Harriet Beecher Stowe at the White House during the Civil War, he said, "So this is the little woman who wrote the book that made this great war."

5.   Though the Free Soil party received few votes in the election of 1848, it had a great effect. The party was formed to keep slavery out of new areas. Its slogan was "Free Soil, Free Speech, Free Labor, and Free Men." In 1848, the Free Soil party nominated former President Martin Van Buren. Van Buren received only 10 percent of the votes and did not win a majority in any state. But Van Buren did win the votes of the abolitionists. These generally would have gone to the Democrats. Because of this, the Whig candidate became President. The Free Soil party was also important in the congressional race. The House of Representatives was almost evenly divided between Whig and Democratic members. The twelve Free Soil members held the balance of power between the two major parties. This made them much stronger than their number would suggest.

3 Disagreements over Slavery

Getting the Main Idea

Read each paragraph below. Choose which of the three sentences following each paragraph best states the main idea of that paragraph. Write the letter of that sentence in the blank.

_____ 1. In the 1840s, both the Democrats and Whigs were divided over what to do about slavery. Some Democrats, known as Barnburners, were against the spread of slavery into new parts of the country. Other Democrats, known as Hunkers, were willing to accept the spread of slavery. The Whigs were also divided over this question. Those who were against the spread of slavery were called Conscience Whigs. Those who were for the spread of slavery were called Cotton Whigs.
  A. Barnburners and Hunkers were both in favor of ending slavery.
  B. Both the Democrats and Whigs disagreed about slavery.
  C. Hunkers and Conscience Whigs believed in the same thing.

_____ 2. The United States gained much new land from Mexico after the Mexican War. In the years before 1850, Congress tried to decide if the new territories would be free or slave. People in the South wanted these territories to become slave states. People in the North wanted them to become free states. Congress somehow had to find a plan that both groups would accept. A part of the Compromise of 1850 known as popular sovereignty took care of the problem. This plan let each territory decide for itself if it would be free or slave.
  A. Northerners wanted the new territories to become slave states.
  B. Popular sovereignty meant that all new territories would become free states.
  C. Popular sovereignty let each territory decide if it would accept slavery.

_____ 3. Another part of the Compromise of 1850 was known as the Fugitive Slave Law. This law ordered citizens to aid in the return of escaped slaves. The slaves were to be taken before a federal judge. They were not given the right to testify. After this hearing, they were returned to their owners. People in the North were opposed to this law. The Anthony Burns case shows the strength of northern resistance to the Fugitive Slave Law. In 1854, Burns escaped from slavery and went to Boston by boat. He was soon discovered by a slave hunter, who wanted Burns sent back to his owner. The people of Boston gathered at the jail where Burns was being held. They refused to let the slave hunters remove him. United States soldiers as well as local police were needed to hold back the crowd of 50,000 people. It cost over $20,000 and the life of one marshal before Burns was finally returned to his owner.
  A. The Anthony Burns case shows the unpopularity of the Fugitive Slave Law.
  B. The Fugitive Slave Law was passed to help slaves escape.
  C. The people of Boston demanded that Anthony Burns be returned to slavery.

_____ 4. In 1854, Congress passed the Kansas-Nebraska Act. This act formed the territories of Kansas and Nebraska from the rest of the Louisiana Purchase. The question of slavery was to be settled by popular sovereignty. That is, the people of each territory would vote to decide if they wanted to become a free or slave state. Groups both for and against slavery moved to Kansas to try to gain power. Fighting broke out between the two groups. A small war began when proslavery and antislavery groups attacked each other's settlements. Kansas soon became known as "bleeding Kansas." The Kansas-Nebraska Act had been intended to settle the slavery question quietly. But in Kansas it led to violence.
  A. Kansas became a free state, and Nebraska became a slave state.
  B. The Kansas-Nebraska Act led to violence in Kansas.
  C. Popular sovereignty settled the fate of slavery by a vote in Congress.

4 Slave Revolts

Getting the Main Idea

Read each paragraph below. Choose which of the three sentences following each paragraph best states the main idea of that paragraph. Write the letter of that sentence in the blank.

_____ 1. Nat Turner was a black minister who lived in Virginia. Turner believed that God wanted him to help slaves win their freedom by killing their owners. In 1831, he led a bloody slave revolt. Close to sixty whites, many of them women and children, were killed in the three-day uprising. As a result of Turner's revolt and other slave revolts, laws were passed in Southern states putting further controls on slaves, especially those who were preachers. Thus, instead of helping slaves in Virginia and other Southern states, Nat Turner's revolt hurt them.
  A. Nat Turner's revolt gained freedom for slaves in Virginia.
  B. Nat Turner was a black minister who lived in Virginia.
  C. Nat Turner's revolt hurt the slaves instead of helping them.

_____ 2. In some parts of the South, there were ten times as many slaves as whites. Because they were outnumbered, slave owners feared that slaves might revolt. Laws known as slave codes were passed in the South to reduce the danger of slave uprisings. These slave codes set up strict rules about how slaves should behave. They made it illegal for slaves to leave the plantation without a pass from their owner. Slaves were not allowed to gather in groups of more than three. At night they had to carry a lighted lantern. They were not allowed to own weapons. Many other rules were included in the slave codes.
  A. Slave codes protected the rights of slaves from cruel masters.
  B. Slaves were greatly outnumbered in parts of the South.
  C. Slave codes were passed to prevent slave revolts.

_____ 3. John Brown was an abolitionist who believed that violence had to be used to end slavery. He also thought it was God's will that he should stop the further spread of slavery. In 1854, Brown went to the Kansas Territory to keep it from becoming a slave state. There, he killed five innocent settlers who favored slavery. After the bloody fighting in Kansas, Brown began planning a slave revolt. In 1859, he went to Virginia. He wanted to give weapons to the slaves there and help them fight for their freedom. He then hoped to set up a separate black state of freed slaves in the mountains of western Virginia. In order to get guns and ammunition, Brown and his followers broke into an arsenal at Harpers Ferry, Virginia, where the government's weapons were stored. Brown's plan failed. He was finally captured, tried for treason, and hanged.
  A. John Brown used violent methods to try to end slavery.
  B. John Brown was the governor of West Virginia.
  C. John Brown was a gun thief.

_____ 4. Henry "Box" Brown gained his freedom in an unusual way. Brown was a slave who worked in his master's tobacco factory in Richmond, Virginia. One day while working at the loading dock of the factory, he planned his escape. The next day, he had a friend nail him inside one of the large wooden shipping crates. The box was then addressed to an antislavery society in Philadelphia. When the box arrived twenty-six hours later, Brown jumped out to claim his freedom. As a free man, Brown gave talks all over the North about his escape.
  A. Henry Brown owned a tobacco factory.
  B. Henry Brown escaped from slavery in an unusual way.
  C. Henry Brown became famous by giving lectures on slavery.

5 Abolition

Learning the Vocabulary

Unscramble the words in capital letters in each of the sentences below. Write your answers in the blanks at the bottom of the page.

1. The **LITIOBANOSIST** were a group of Americans who worked to end slavery.

2. The **IRENACAM NOOCITOLAZIN EICOSYT** was an organization that helped free slaves and send them to Africa.

3. The **RGREDNUDNUO LIARDAOR** was a network of hiding places by which slaves escaped from the South.

4. **EITRAHR BMUATN** was the most famous conductor on the underground railroad. She helped about three hundred slaves escape.

5. The political party named the **REFE LOIS YRAPT** was formed to help stop the spread of slavery into new territories.

6. **HONJ WONRB** was an abolitionist who used violence to try to end slavery. He was captured and hung for treason.

7. **REITARH ECEBREH WTOES** wrote *Uncle Tom's Cabin.*

8. **IMLALWI ISNOARGR** published the famous abolitionist newspaper *The Liberator.*

9. **SPRAREH YERFR** was the United States arsenal in Virginia where John Brown and his followers tried unsuccessfully to steal guns.

10. **CIREKERDF SGLUOSAD** was an escaped slave who became a famous abolitionist speaker.

1. _____   6. _____

2. _____   7. _____

3. _____   8. _____

4. _____   9. _____

5. _____   10. _____

6 Problems over Slavery

Learning the Vocabulary

Read each sentence below. Then complete the sentence by filling in the spaces correctly. Each dash represents one letter in the correct spelling of the word.

1. _ _ _   _ _ _ _ _ _ _ was the inventor of the cotton gin.

2. The _ _ _ _ _ _ _ _ _ _   _ _   _ _ _ _ was a bill passed by Congress which included

   the principle of popular sovereignty. This bill also included the Fugitive Slave Law.

3. _ _ _ _ _ _ _   _ _ _ _ _ _ _ _ _ _ _ was a plan that allowed a territory to decide for

   itself whether or not to permit slavery.

4. The _ _ _ _ _ _   _ _ _ was a machine for removing the seeds in cotton quickly. This inven-

   tion made cotton growing a profitable industry.

5. The _ _ _ _ _   _ _ _ _ _ were laws that regulated the behavior of slaves in the southern

   states.

6. _ _ _   _ _ _ _ _ _ led a slave revolt in 1831. Frightened by this revolt, lawmakers in

   Virginia voted against ending slavery.

7. _ _ _ _ _   _ _ _ _ _ was a slave who had himself shipped in a box to Philadelphia, Pennsyl-

   vania, to gain his freedom.

8. _ _ _ _ _ _   _ _ _ _ _ _ _ _ _ was a southern author who wrote in defense of slavery.

9. The _ _ _ _ _ _ _ _   _ _ _ _ _   _ _ _ required northerners to return all runaway

   slaves to their owners.

10. _ _ _ _ _ _ _   _ _ _ _ _ was an escaped slave who reached Boston, Massachusetts. His

    capture and return to slavery caused a major riot in Boston.

7 People and Places

Learning the Vocabulary

Fill in the squares to spell out the names or terms described in the clues.

ACROSS
3. Abolitionist who used violence to try to end slavery
4. Author of *Uncle Tom's Cabin*
7. People who wanted to end slavery
10. Leader of a slave revolt in 1831

DOWN
1. Publisher of an abolitionist newspaper
2. Escaped slave who became a famous abolitionist speaker
5. Inventor of the cotton gin
6. African colony set up to receive freed blacks from the United States
8. Escaped slave whose return to slavery caused a riot in Boston
9. Conductor on the underground railroad

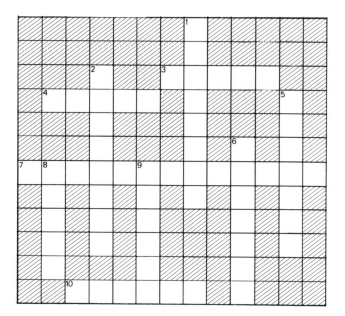

8 Heading Toward Civil War

Learning the Vocabulary

The following words have been used in the main idea section. See if you can find these words in the word search puzzle below. Circle them. They may be found vertically or horizontally. They may also overlap.

abolitionists	Whitney
Tubman	cotton gin
Liberia	slave codes
Brown	Turner
Harpers Ferry	Fitzhugh
Stowe	Burns
Free Soil party	Fugitive Slave Law
Garrison	*Uncle Tom's Cabin*

```
F  U  G  I  T  I  V  E  S  L  A  V  E  L  A  W
R  C  A  A  F  C  M  F  L  I  B  T  T  B  O  T
E  D  R  C  C  D  N  I  A  B  O  C  B  D  T  U
E  L  R  D  X  F  V  T  V  E  L  X  U  T  W  R
S  O  I  I  C  L  O  Z  E  R  I  V  R  O  M  N
O  E  S  T  O  W  E  H  C  I  T  Z  N  V  N  E
I  D  O  U  A  H  B  U  O  A  I  Q  S  C  M  R
L  F  N  B  B  I  R  G  D  P  O  O  X  O  I  C
P  L  P  M  D  T  O  H  E  L  N  N  Q  T  N  X
A  C  Q  A  P  N  W  X  S  M  I  L  Z  T  W  B
R  A  C  N  E  N  C  D  C  S  C  G  O  X  L
T  X  I  R  X  Y  T  O  X  O  T  A  A  N  C  M
Y  O  B  O  Z  T  C  V  C  N  S  F  L  G  D  A
H  A  R  P  E  R  S  F  E  R  R  Y  M  I  I  H
U  N  C  L  E  T  O  M  S  C  A  B  I  N  B  O
```

9 Railroad Mileage, 1830–1860

Reading Maps and Graphs

New means of transportation made it easier for people to settle in the West. Study the line graph on railroads below and then answer the questions that follow.

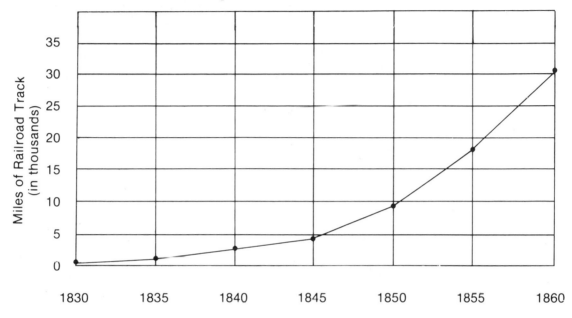

1. What do the numbers on the left side of the graph represent? _____

_____

2. What do the numbers across the bottom of the graph represent? _____

3. How many years does the graph cover? _____

4. Did the amount of railroad track increase or decrease during these years? _____

5. During which five-year period was the most railroad track constructed? _____

6. During which five-year period was the least amount of railroad track constructed? _____

7. Was the greatest amount of track constructed before or after 1845? _____

8. Approximately how many miles of track were built before 1845? _____

_____

9. Approximately how many miles of track were built between 1845 and 1860? _____

_____

10. What was the total amount of track laid during this entire period? _____

_____

10 Selected Cities, 1800-1860

Reading Maps and Graphs

Study the map and chart below and then answer the following questions.

Population of Selected Cities

	1800	1810	1820	1830	1840	1850	1860
New York	79,216	119,734	152,056	242,278	391,114	696,115	1,174,779
Philadelphia	41,220	53,722	63,802	80,462	93,665	121,376	565,529
Savannah, Ga.	5,146	5,215	7,523	7,303	11,214	15,312	22,292
Cleveland	—	—	606	1,076	6,071	17,034	43,417
Chicago	—	—	—	—	4,470	29,963	112,172
San Francisco	—	—	—	—	—	34,776	56,802
Houston	—	—	—	—	—	2,396	4,845

1. Which city shown had the greatest population growth from 1800 to 1860? _____

2. What section of the United States contained the most populous cities in 1800? _____

3. How many of the cities mentioned above did not show a population in 1810? Name them.

_____

4. In what general direction are these cities from the Atlantic Coast? _____

5. In what section of the United States is Savannah located? _____

6. In 1810, Savannah was the third largest city shown. How did it rank in 1860? _____

7. What city shown ranked third in population in 1860? _____

8. In what section of the country is this city located? _____

9. What city shown ranked fourth in 1860? _____

10. In what section of the country is this city located? _____

11 Public Land Sales, 1800–1860

Reading Maps and Graphs

In the nineteenth century, the United States greatly increased its land holdings. The government sold most of this public land to people who, for one reason or another, wished to move to the western sections of the United States. Study the graph and answer the questions.

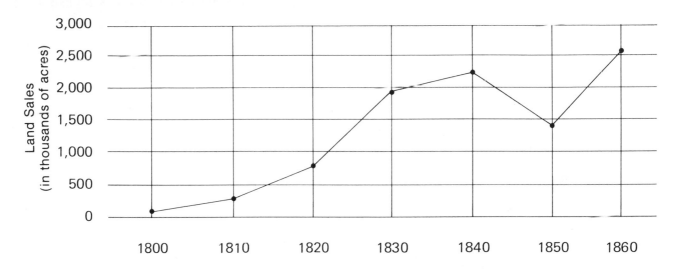

1. Did public land sales generally increase or decrease between 1800 and 1860? _____

2. Which ten-year period experienced a decrease in sales over the previous ten-year period?

_____

3. In which ten-year period was the increase in land sales the smallest? _____

4. In which ten-year period did land sales reach the highest point shown on the graph?

_____

5. Can you determine from the graph that much of the public land sold was located in the West?

_____

12 Slavery in the United States

Readings Maps and Graphs

As you have read, Eli Whitney's invention of the cotton gin increased the demand for slaves to work on southern plantations. Most of the slaves were blacks who had been brought from Africa. However, not all blacks were slaves. Some blacks lived in the North, where slavery had been outlawed. There were also a number of nonslave blacks in the South during the 1800s. Study the graph below and answer the questions.

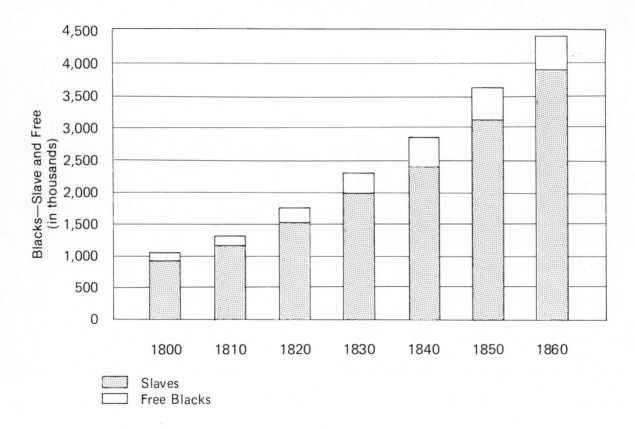

1. Did slavery increase or decrease between 1800 and 1860? _____

2. Which ten-year period saw the largest increase in the number of slaves? _____

3. Approximately how many blacks were in the United States in 1860? How many of these were

slaves? _____

_____

4. How many more slaves were there in 1860 than in 1840? _____

5. Did the number of free blacks increase or decrease between 1800 and 1860? _____

1 Secession

Getting the Main Idea

Read each paragraph below. Choose which of the three sentences following each paragraph best states the main idea of that paragraph. Write the letter of that sentence in the blank.

_____ 1. The United States was badly divided by the election of 1860. Four men ran for President. None of them agreed on slavery. The Democratic party split into two branches over this question. The northern branch ran Stephen Douglas. He believed that popular sovereignty should decide the matter of bringing slaves into the territories. The southern branch ran John Breckinridge. He favored the spread of slavery. The man running for the Constitutional Union party took no stand on the question at all. The candidate of the Republican party was Abraham Lincoln. Though Lincoln accepted slavery where it was present already, he was against letting it spread into the territories. Lincoln won the election. But his victory showed how badly the country was divided. He won in every free state but lost in every slave state.

    A. The election of 1860 shows how badly the nation was divided over slavery.

    B. Lincoln was very popular in the southern slave states.

    C. The Democrats won the presidential election of 1860.

_____ 2. Before the election of 1860, southern leaders had warned that the South would leave the Union if Lincoln were elected. Several weeks after Lincoln's victory, South Carolina seceded from, or left, the Union. Six other states also voted to secede. In early 1861, these seven states formed their own country, called the Confederate States of America. They drew up their own constitution and chose Jefferson Davis as President. On April 14, 1861, the Confederate army captured the Union's Fort Sumter in South Carolina. The Civil War had begun. Soon afterwards, four more states seceded. The Confederacy then numbered eleven states.

    A. Abraham Lincoln was the leader of the Confederacy.

    B. The southern states seceded from the Union and formed the Confederacy after Lincoln's election.

    C. Jefferson Davis replaced Lincoln as President after the fall of Fort Sumter.

_____ 3. When the Civil War began, people had no idea how terrible the next four years would be. They thought the war would be over soon. Soldiers marched off to battle in brightly colored uniforms. Politicians gave stirring speeches about the great cause they were fighting for. Hundreds of people watched the Battle of Bull Run near Washington, D.C. Some even packed picnic lunches. After the battle, the bodies of the dead and the wounded littered the ground. Only then did people begin to realize how terrible war can be.

    A. The Civil War ended at the Battle of Bull Run.

    B. Right from the start, people knew that the Civil War would be terrible.

    C. At first, people did not take the Civil War seriously.

_____ 4. At the beginning of the Civil War, Robert E. Lee had to choose between his love for the Union and his love for his state of Virginia. It was a very difficult decision for him. Lee was against slavery and the breaking up of the Union. He had served in the United States army for thirty-two years. President Lincoln even offered him command of the Union army. But Lee did not feel that he could fight against his home state. He resigned from the army. Later Lee accepted the command of the Army of Northern Virginia. He went on to become the greatest general of the Confederacy.

    A. Robert E. Lee fought for the Union during the Civil War.

    B. The Civil War forced Robert E. Lee to decide between his country and his state.

    C. Robert E. Lee was the least able of the Confederate generals.

2 Civil War

Getting the Main Idea

Read each paragraph below. Then underline the sentence that best states the main idea of each paragraph.

1. Though Lincoln's major reason for fighting the Civil War was to save the Union, an important result of the war was freedom for the slaves. Lincoln was against slavery, but he did not believe at first that he had the power to end it. When the abolitionists tried to push him to free the slaves early in the war, Lincoln would not do so. But as the war went on, Lincoln changed his mind. Freedom for the slaves was the cause he needed to keep the North together and win support from Europe. He could also justify freeing the slaves as a war measure against the South. In 1863, Lincoln set forth his Emancipation Proclamation. This act freed only the slaves in those parts of the South still fighting against the Union. It did not free slaves in those slave states that had stayed loyal to the North. Nor did it free slaves in those parts of the South held by northern armies. Slavery in all the states was at last ended in 1865, when Congress passed the Thirteenth Amendment to the Constitution.

2. The North had many advantages over the South at the beginning of the Civil War. The North was much larger than the South. It had twenty-three states, while the South had only eleven states. The North also had three times as many people as the South. The North could more easily produce and ship the supplies needed for war. It had over 90 percent of the country's factories and 70 percent of the country's railroads. The North was better able to pay for the war. It had strong banks and 70 percent of the country's wealth. The North produced more food than the South. It had 65 percent of the country's farms.

3. The Civil War was the first modern war in history. New kinds of weapons and military strategies were used for the first time. Trench warfare took the place of hand-to-hand fighting. Rifles were more accurate, and cannons had a greater range. A form of the machine gun was used during this war. War at sea was also different. Submarines appeared for the first time. A battle between the *Monitor* and the *Merrimac* marked the first use of armored ships. Other devices were also first used in time of war. Hot-air balloons helped in the observation of enemy troops, and the telegraph speeded up communications.

4. The Battle of Shiloh was the bloodiest battle ever fought in North America up to that time. There were more casualties at Shiloh than in all the battles of the Revolutionary War, the War of 1812, and the Mexican War together. Over 100,000 soldiers fought in this battle, which took place in southwest Tennessee on April 6 and 7, 1862. One-fourth of the Confederate soldiers and one-third of the Union soldiers taking part in the Battle of Shiloh were killed, wounded, or taken prisoner. The Union lost 13,000 men, and the Confederates lost over 10,000 men. The South also lost the head of their army, General Albert S. Johnson, who bled to death after receiving a leg wound.

5. General William T. Sherman's march to the sea caused great destruction. From November to December 1864, Sherman led 600,000 men on a three-hundred-mile (480 kilometers) march from Atlanta, Georgia, to the seaport of Savannah. Sherman wanted to make the state of Georgia "an example to rebels." His men took all the food and loot they wanted and then destroyed what was left. As they marched toward Savannah, they left a path of ruins behind them sixty miles (96 kilometers) wide. Railroad tracks were ripped up. The rails were turned into "Sherman's hairpins" by heating them in fires and then bending them around trees and telegraph poles. Factories and warehouses were destroyed. Bridges were blown up. Crops were burned. Over 100,000 horses and mules were captured.

3 Political Problems

Getting the Main Idea

Read each paragraph below. Then write what you think is the main idea of each paragraph on the lines provided.

1.   When the Civil War began, the North depended on volunteers for soldiers. But soon men stopped volunteering. The army had a hard time finding soldiers to take the place of the dead and wounded. In 1863, Congress passed the country's first draft law, the Conscription Act. This act was unfair and unpopular. Under this law, a man could get out of being drafted by paying $300. A poor man who could not pay would have to join the army. In some northern cities, riots broke out over the Conscription Act. A riot in New York lasted for three days. Over one million dollars in property was destroyed. Forty people were killed, and over one thousand were injured.

The main idea of this paragraph is _____

_____

2.   The state of West Virginia was formed because part of the state of Virginia did not want to secede from the Union. When the Civil War began, Virginia voted to leave the Union. The people in the forty-eight counties in the western corner of Virginia did not want to secede. They did not own slaves and did not want to fight a war to protect slavery. Instead, they voted to remain part of the United States. In 1863, West Virginia joined the Union as a free state.

The main idea of this paragraph is _____

_____

3.   President Lincoln thought he would have a hard time winning reelection in 1864. By that time the country was very tired of war. The fighting had dragged on for over three years, and victory was still not in sight. Many people in the North blamed Lincoln for not bringing the war to an end. Unhappy leaders in the Republican party wanted to replace him with another candidate. They were afraid that their party would lose if Lincoln ran. Lincoln did win the election, but he received only 55 percent of the popular vote.

The main idea of this paragraph is _____

_____

4.   The Confederate states often did not agree with each other during the Civil War. States' rights, a major reason for secession, soon caused great problems. Several southern states placed their own interests above those of the Confederacy. North Carolina and Georgia refused to send their share of soldiers to the Confederate army. They also did not share their war supplies with the rest of the states. Even the government had troubles. Many of those in high office openly found fault with President Jefferson Davis. Alexander H. Stephens, the Vice-President, even tried to make a separate peace with the Union.

The main idea of this paragraph is _____

_____

4 Reconstruction

Getting the Main Idea

Read each paragraph below. Choose which of the three sentences following each paragraph best states the main idea of that paragraph. Write the letter of that sentence in the blank.

_____ 1. The period after the Civil War is known as Reconstruction. During that time, it was important to heal the South and restore it to the Union. Thousands of miles of railroad tracks had to be repaired. Towns and cities destroyed during the war had to be rebuilt. Slave owners had to find new workers to take the place of the freed slaves. The defeated southern states also had to form new governments before they could join the Union again.
  A. The South had to be rebuilt and restored to the Union during Reconstruction.
  B. Reconstruction was involved with the physical repairs of the North.
  C. The Civil War ended at the Battle of Reconstruction.

_____ 2. The presidential and congressional plans for reconstruction were very different. President Lincoln, and later President Johnson, planned to allow the southern states to return to the Union without punishing them. All but a few of the southern leaders would be pardoned after taking a loyalty oath. Part of this oath was a promise to obey laws dealing with slavery. On the other hand, leaders in Congress known as the Radical Republicans wanted to punish the South severely. They planned to take the right to vote away from anyone who had served in the southern army or government. The southern states would have to meet certain requirements before they could come back into the Union. The congressional plan centered much of its attention on the freed slaves. It demanded equal rights for blacks.
  A. The presidential and congressional plans for Reconstruction were very much alike.
  B. The presidential and congressional plans for Reconstruction were not alike.
  C. When Johnson became President, he threw out Lincoln's plan for reconstruction.

_____ 3. On April 14, 1865, only five days after the end of the Civil War, President Lincoln was shot and killed by John Wilkes Booth. Booth believed that Lincoln was an enemy of the South and that the South would be better off with him dead. Booth was wrong. Instead of helping the South, the assassination of Lincoln harmed the South. Lincoln had wanted to heal the wounds caused by the war. He had intended that the southern states be treated leniently. Some people in the North believed that southern leaders were behind Lincoln's murder. This idea helped the Radical Republicans. They pushed harder for treating the South harshly.
  A. President Lincoln wanted to punish the South for causing the Civil War.
  B. Lincoln's death hurt the South instead of helping it.
  C. John Wilkes Booth was a great admirer of President Lincoln.

_____ 4. In 1867, Congress passed a number of harsh laws known as the Reconstruction acts. The South was divided into five districts. Each district was ruled by an army officer, backed up by soldiers. These acts also ordered the defeated southern states to meet certain demands before they could escape army rule and join the Union again. The southern states had to form constitutions giving blacks the right to vote. Only citizens who took an oath that they had never willingly aided the Confederacy were allowed to take part in writing these constitutions. Southern states also had to accept the Fourteenth Amendment. This law gave equal rights to blacks.
  A. The Reconstruction acts set up state governments in the South.
  B. The Reconstruction acts welcomed the South into the Union at once.
  C. The Reconstruction acts were very harsh.

5 Problems of Reconstruction

Getting the Main Idea

Read each paragraph below. Then write what you think is the main idea of each paragraph on the lines provided.

1. President Andrew Johnson did his best to keep Congress from carrying out its reconstruction plans. This angered the Radical Republicans. They began to look for an excuse to remove him from office. In 1867, Congress passed the Tenure of Office Act. Under this act, the President had to get the Senate's approval before he fired any high government officers. It was intended to trap him into breaking the law. In 1868, Johnson fired Secretary of War Edward Stanton. The House of Representatives brought impeachment charges against Johnson. When Johnson was tried before the Senate, it became clear that he had not done anything illegal. Johnson was really impeached because he did not agree with Congress.

The main idea of this paragraph is _____

_____

2. After the war, some northern Republicans moved south to take part in southern politics. These people were called carpetbaggers. Some of them were very crooked. Many received huge salaries on which they paid no taxes. They used state money to buy luxuries. South Carolina even paid back one lawmaker for the thousand dollars he had lost on a horse race. Some carpetbaggers sold their votes. Several southern states were put into debt after state money was given to companies for railroads and canals which were never built.

The main idea of this paragraph is _____

_____

3. After the war, anyone who had served in the Confederate army or government was not allowed to vote or hold public office. This kept most whites out of government. Blacks, who had just been given the right to vote, began to hold office. To stop blacks from taking over the South, southern whites formed the Ku Klux Klan. The Klan tried to keep blacks from voting or taking government jobs. It warned blacks that they would be hurt or murdered if they did not obey the Klan. Many times, Klan members beat or lynched the blacks or burned their houses.

The main idea of this paragraph is _____

_____

4. After the slaves were freed, they faced terrible hardships. They had no homes, food, or jobs. In 1865, over 100,000 ex-slaves died of starvation or disease. At last, the government stepped in and set up the Freedmen's Bureau to help these freed slaves. The Bureau gave them food and clothing. It helped them find jobs. It also gave them free legal advice. Since slaves had not been allowed to read or write, the Bureau built schools and started classes for them.

The main idea of this paragraph is _____

_____

6   Divided Nation

Learning the Vocabulary

Read each sentence below. Then complete the sentence by filling in the spaces correctly. Each dash represents one letter in the correct spelling of the word.

1. _ _ _ _ _ _ _   _ _ _ _ _ _ was the Republican candidate in the presidential election of

   1860. He won the election and thus was President during the Civil War.

2. Stephen Douglas, the northern Democratic candidate in the election of 1860, believed that

   _ _ _ _ _ _ _   _ _ _ _ _ _ _ _ _ _ _ should decide the question of slavery in the

   territories.

3. _ _ _ _ _   _ _ _ _ _ _ _ _ was the first southern state to leave the Union.

4. After the election of 1860, the _ _ _ _ _ _ _ _ _ of southern states from the Union led to

   the formation of the Confederacy.

5. The _ _ _ _ _ _ _ _ _ _ _   _ _ _ _ _ _   _ _   _ _ _ _ _ _ _ was the name of the

   nation that was formed when the southern states broke away from the Union.

6. _ _ _ _ _ _ _ _ _   _ _ _ _ _ was the President of the Confederate States of America

   during the Civil War.

7. The state of _ _ _ _   _ _ _ _ _ _ _ _ was formed when people in the western part of

   Virginia decided not to leave the Union along with the rest of the state.

8. The Confederate army attacked the federal garrison at _ _ _ _   _ _ _ _ _ _ in April 1861.

   This was the beginning of the Civil War.

9. The _ _ _ _ _ _   _ _   _ _ _ _   _ _ _, which was fought near Washington, D.C.,

   opened the eyes of many people to the fact that the war was going to be long and costly.

10. _ _ _ _ _ _   _   _ _ _ was the South's greatest general during the Civil War.

7 The Conduct of the War

Learning the Vocabulary

Unscramble the words in capital letters in each of the sentences below. Write your answers in the blanks at the bottom of the page.

1. **MALILWI RMENASH** destroyed a great deal of property as he marched across the state of Georgia from Atlanta to the port of Savannah.

2. The **LBATET FO LSIHHO** was the bloodiest conflict of the Civil War.

3. An important result of the Civil War was freedom for the **VALSES**.

4. **RFOT TRMUES** was attacked by the Confederate army in April 1861. This signaled the beginning of the Civil War.

5. The **INENOAMCTPIA LCNORPMAOIAT** was President Lincoln's order to free all slaves in the southern states that were still in rebellion.

6. In many northern cities, bloody **STIOR** were fought over the Conscription Act in 1863.

7. The **NTERITTEHH TDANEMNEM** stated that slavery was outlawed everywhere in the United States.

8. The **ATBTEL FO ULBL NRU** was fought near Washington, D.C., and was one of the first clases between the Confederate and Union armies.

9. The **NSNOOCRICIPT CAT** was the first draft law in the nation's history. This law, passed in 1863, was an unfair and unpopular law.

10. The **RNOITMO** and **IRCEMAMR** were the first armored ships to battle during a war.

1. _____   6. _____

2. _____   7. _____

3. _____   8. _____

4. _____   9. _____

5. _____   10. _____

8 Reconstruction Years

Learning the Vocabulary

Fill in the blank in each of the following sentences with the word that best fits. Use each word in the list below just once.

Reconstruction acts	Radical Republicans
Freedmen's Bureau	Reconstruction
carpetbaggers	Tenure of Office Act
Ku Klux Klan	Andrew Johnson
John Wilkes Booth	Fourteenth Amendment

1. The _____ helped to provide food, clothing, and jobs for the blacks after the Civil War.

2. _____ became President of the United States after Abraham Lincoln was shot and killed. He also was the only President of the United States to be impeached.

3. The _____ was a secret organization formed by southern whites to keep blacks from controlling their state governments.

4. _____ refers to the period after the Civil War when the South was rebuilt and readmitted to the Union.

5. The _____ were congressmen who thought the Lincoln-Johnson plan for restoring the Union was too easy on the South.

6. The _____ were northerners who held government posts in the South during the Reconstruction period. These men usually carried bags made of carpet.

7. The _____ divided the South into military districts and set up strict rules for how the southern states could be readmitted to the Union.

8. _____ was the man who shot President Abraham Lincoln at Ford's Theater on April 14, 1865.

9. The _____ was the law used by the Radical Republicans to impeach President Andrew Johnson. The law stated that the President must get approval from the Senate before he could fire any of his officials.

10. The _____ guaranteed equal right for blacks.

9 People, Places, and Things

Learning the Vocabulary

Match the vocabulary words on the left with the meanings on the right. Write the correct letter in the blank next to the vocabulary word.

_____ 1. Radical Republicans

_____ 2. secession

_____ 3. Ku Klux Klan

_____ 4. Thirteenth Amendment

_____ 5. presidential reconstruction

_____ 6. carpetbaggers

_____ 7. John Wilkes Booth

_____ 8. Freedmen's Bureau

_____ 9. congressional reconstruction

_____ 10. Battle of Shiloh

_____ 11. William Sherman

_____ 12. Andrew Johnson

_____ 13. Jefferson Davis

_____ 14. Robert E. Lee

_____ 15. Abraham Lincoln

_____ 16. Edward Stanton

_____ 17. Emancipation Proclamation

_____ 18. Fourteenth Amendment

_____ 19. South Carolina

_____ 20. Confederate States of America

A. First southern state to secede from the Union
B. Secretary of War during Johnson's presidency
C. Breaking away from the Union by many southern states after the election of 1860
D. Man who shot President Lincoln
E. Bloodiest battle of the Civil War
F. Leading Confederate commander
G. President Lincoln's order to free slaves in Confederate territories still at war
H. Organization formed to help the newly freed slaves
I. Plan for rebuilding the South that was favored by Congress
J. Northerners who went south during Reconstruction to take part in politics
K. Change in the Constitution that gave blacks equal rights
L. Plan for rebuilding the nation that was favored by Lincoln and Johnson
M. Name of the nation that seceded from the Union
N. President of the United States during the Civil War
O. Northern commander who destroyed everything of value in his advance through Georgia
P. Congressmen who wanted to be harsh with southern states after the Civil War
Q. Change in the Constitution that ended slavery
R. President of the Confederate States of America
S. Group of white southerners who used violence towards blacks
T. President of the United States who was impeached

10 Secession, 1860–1861

Reading Maps and Graphs

The surrender of Fort Sumter to Confederate troops on April 14, 1861, marked the beginning of the Civil War. The map below shows the slave states that seceded from the Union before April 14, 1861, those that seceded after that date, those slave states that never seceded (called border states), and the free states. Study the map and answer the following questions.

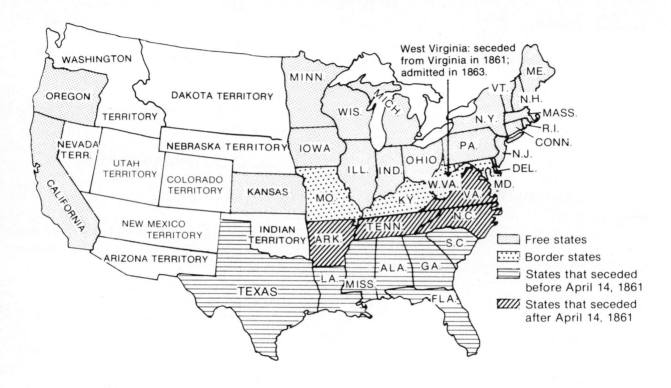

1. How many states seceded before April 14, 1861? List them. _____

_____

2. How many states seceded after April 14, 1861? List them. _____

_____

3. How many border states are shown? List them. _____

_____

4. How many free states existed at the time the southern states seceded? _____

5. Was the state in which you now live a Union, Confederate, or border state? Or was your state not a

state at the time of the Civil War? _____

_____

11 Election of 1860

Reading Maps and Graphs

Study the map below. Then answer the questions that follow. Use the map on page 70, if necessary, to answer the questions.

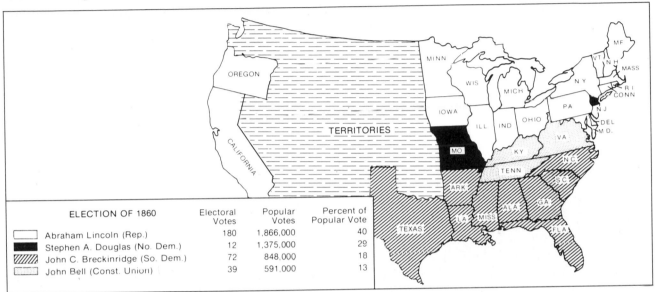

ELECTION OF 1860	Electoral Votes	Popular Votes	Percent of Popular Vote
Abraham Lincoln (Rep.)	180	1,866,000	40
Stephen A. Douglas (No. Dem.)	12	1,375,000	29
John C. Breckinridge (So. Dem.)	72	848,000	18
John Bell (Const. Union)	39	591,000	13

1. Which party had two candidates in this election? _____

2. What were the names of these two candidates? _____

_____

3. Which candidate won this election? _____

4. What percentage of the popular vote did the winner receive? _____

5. How many electoral votes did the winner receive? _____

6. Which candidate carried the fewest states? _____

7. Which candidate carried the most free states? _____

8. Which candidate carried the most slave states? _____

9. What states did Bell carry? _____

10. What state split its vote between two candidates? _____

12 Civil War Deaths

Reading Maps and Graphs

Study the graph below. Then answer the questions that follow.

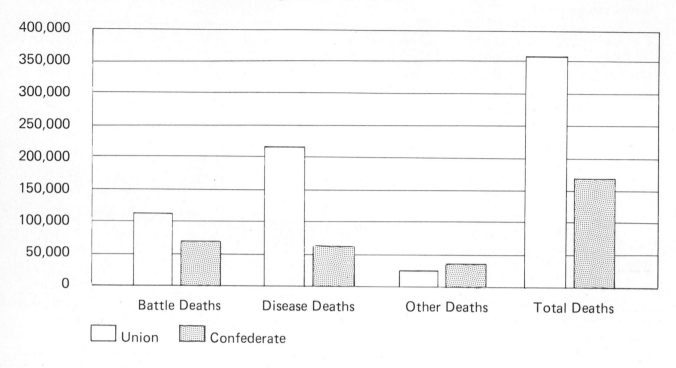

1. What caused most of the deaths in the Civil War? _____

2. What were the total number of battle deaths for both sides during the war? _____

_____

3. Which side suffered the largest number of battle deaths during the war? _____

4. What were the total number of deaths for both sides during the war? _____

_____

5. Which side had more than twice as many total deaths as the other? _____

1 Settling the West

Getting the Main Idea

Read each paragraph below. Then underline the sentence that best states the main idea of each paragraph.

1.   Jim Bridger, a famous mountain man and guide, was very important to the settlement of the West. He helped discover, explore, and settle the Rocky Mountain region. On the first of his many expeditions into the western wilderness, Bridger explored the Missouri River. On another trip, he discovered the South Pass, which later proved to be the best route across the Rocky Mountains. Because he knew so much about the western territories and the Indians who lived there, Bridger became a guide for wagon trains along the Oregon Trail. In 1843, he built a trading post and way station along the Oregon Trail. This post, Fort Bridger, was one of the first permanent settlements in Wyoming.

2.   The Mormons moved west to escape religious persecution. The Church of Jesus Christ of Latter-Day Saints, better known as the Mormon Church, was founded by Joseph Smith in 1830 in New York. From the beginning, the Mormons were harassed by others who did not understand their religion. Seeking a place where they could worship in peace, the Mormons moved first to Ohio and Missouri and then settled in Illinois. But the Mormons were persecuted in Illinois also. It was there that Smith was murdered in 1844 while being held in jail. The Mormon settlement of Nauvoo, Illinois, was raided and burned. The new Mormon leader, Brigham Young, knew that the Mormons could not remain in Illinois. In 1847, he led them westward to find an isolated area where they could worship as they pleased. At last they settled on the shores of the Great Salt Lake in Utah, where they founded Salt Lake City.

3.   Wagon trains moving west sometimes faced great dangers, as the fate of the Donner party proves. In late spring of 1846, eighty-nine settlers led by George Donner headed for California. By late summer, the Donner party was far behind schedule. They still had several mountain ranges to cross. When they finally reached the mountains in October, the passes were blocked by heavy snowfall. The Donner party was trapped in the mountains until the snow melted in the spring. Their food and other supplies were quickly used up. Many of the settlers starved or froze to death. Others stayed alive only by eating the flesh of those who had died. When the snow melted, only forty-nine of the settlers were rescued.

4.   Many different groups helped settle the West. Chinese and Irish workers helped build the railroads which opened the West. Many stayed on to farm or to work in the towns. After the end of slavery, many blacks went west to work on ranches and cattle trails. As many as one-third of the cowboys were former slaves. Nat Love was the best-known of these black cowboys. There were also black lawmen, miners, farmers, and soldiers. The Spanish were also important to the settlement of the West. The Spanish taught the Americans about raising cattle, mining, and farming. The rodeo, branding iron, and lasso were all introduced by the Spanish.

5.   The United States government helped western settlement by selling land cheaply or giving it away free. Under one act passed in 1841, a settler could buy up to 160 acres (64.8 hectares) of government land for only $1.25 an acre. The Homestead Act of 1862 gave 160 acres to any settler who would live on the land and farm it for five years. After the Civil War, a Union veteran with four years military service or his widow could get 160 acres free by living on it for one year. Another act in 1873 gave settlers 160 acres if they agreed to plant trees on the land. The largest and last government giveaway was on April 22, 1889. Nearly 3 million acres of Indian Territory in Oklahoma were opened for settlement. Over twelve thousand homesteads were staked out in the mad scramble known as the Oklahoma Land Rush.

2 Indians

Getting the Main Idea

Read each paragraph below. Then write what you think is the main idea of each paragraph on the lines provided.

1.   The Indians on the western plains depended on the buffalo for their survival. Almost every part of the buffalo was useful to them. They used the sinews to make thread and bowstrings. The horns were used to make cups and spoons. Buffalo hair was braided into belts and ropes. The Indians made their tepees from buffalo hides. The buffalo was most important as a source of food. The Indians killed only as many buffalo as they needed. The Indians' survival became threatened as whites senselessly began to kill the buffalo by the millions. The most famous hunter, William "Buffalo Bill" Cody, killed over five thousand in less than eighteen months.

The main idea of this paragraph is _____

_____

2.   As settlers moved farther west, the Indians were forced off their land. The government then set aside land known as reservations for the Indians. In return for living on these reservations, the Indians were promised food and supplies from the government. Many times, the Indians did not receive supplies as promised. When they moved to the reservations, the Indians had to give up their favorite hunting grounds. They were used to hunting animal herds by following them over large tracts of land. The Indians were never happy living on the reservations.

The main idea of this paragraph is _____

_____

3.   For over four hundred years, the Indians fought to stop the westward advance of white settlers. Though each side won and lost battles, the settlers continued their push into Indian territory. The Battle of the Little Bighorn marked the Indians' last victory of the Indian wars. In June 1876, Lieutenant Colonel George Custer led the 7th Cavalry against an Indian village near the Little Bighorn River in Montana. Eager for victory, Custer underestimated the strength of the Indians. As many as 4,000 Sioux and Cheyenne Indians overwhelmed the soldiers. Less than one hour later, over 260 soldiers at "Custer's Last Stand" were dead.

The main idea of this paragraph is _____

_____

4.   Unhappy with life on the reservation, some Indians turned to the new Ghost Dance religion. These Indians believed that the old days would soon return. The dead who had been killed in battle would be brought back to life. There would be no white settlers. The buffalo would come back. The Indians would again hunt the buffalo, following the herds across miles of open plains. To hasten the return of their old way of life, the Indians danced and sang while wearing special clothes and make-up.

The main idea of this paragraph is _____

_____

3 Cowboys

Getting the Main Idea

Read each paragraph below. Choose which of the three sentences following each paragraph best states the main idea of that paragraph. Write the letter of that sentence in the blank.

_____ 1. The cowboys of the American West were very different from the cowboys that appear today in movie westerns. The life of the real cowboy was not very glamorous. Cowboys spent long, dusty hours riding in a hard saddle. The average working day was between twelve and fifteen hours. Cowboys often did not even own their horses or saddles. They were paid no more than a factory worker. The cowboys' work was dirty, dangerous, and often lonely.
    A. Cowboys of the American West led an exciting and glamorous life.
    B. The cowboys were well paid for their work.
    C. Cowboys in real life did not have a glamorous job.

_____ 2. During the days of the cattle drives, ranchers in Texas sometimes made money and sometimes lost money. Between 1870 and 1890, cattle roamed free on the open range. Once a year they were rounded up and driven along the Chisholm Trail to the railroad station in Abilene, Kansas. In Texas, these cattle were worth only a few dollars. But in the eastern cities, such as St. Louis, they were worth $40 each. By driving their cattle north along the trail to the railroad, ranchers could increase the value of their herds. A $15,000 investment in cattle could easily make a profit of $30,000 in less than one year. However, there were dangers along the trail that could sometimes wipe out a rancher's profits. Indians, rustlers, and diseases claimed many cattle before they reached the market. Bad weather was also a problem. Winter snow storms and spring floods sometimes killed whole herds. Some years all the grass was killed by drought, and the cattle starved.
    A. Texas ranchers sometimes made money and sometimes lost money on the cattle drives.
    B. Cattle were more valuable in Texas than in St. Louis.
    C. The hazards on the cattle trail discouraged ranchers from making any cattle drives.

_____ 3. For many years, cattle in the western states grazed on unfenced government-owned land covering thousands of acres. Later, farmers arrived and began to search for ways to fence in their crop lands. Because there were so few trees, wooden fences were not practical. Ordinary metal wire would not keep out the ranchers' cattle. Finally, in 1874 Joseph Glidden patented barbed wire. It was immediately popular with the western farmers. Within ten years, barbed wire fences had broken up the open range into fields and pastures and blocked the cattle trails.
    A. Wooden fences were better than wire fences.
    B. Barbed wire led to the end of the open range.
    C. Ranchers on the open range protected their trails with barbed wire.

_____ 4. Before the invention of the revolver, cowboys were armed with guns that fired a single shot. This meant that they had to reload every time they fired their guns. The Indians, using bows and arrows, could get off many shots in the time it took a cowboy to load his gun. Under these conditions, the Indians had the advantage. However, with the invention of the Colt revolver, the odds changed in favor of the cowboy. These guns had rotating chambers which held six rounds of ammunition. The cowboy could now fire six bullets as fast as he could pull the trigger.
    A. The Indians were better shots than the cowboys.
    B. The revolver shifted the odds in favor of the cowboys and against the Indians.
    C. Bows and arrows were a better weapon than the revolver.

4   Mining

Getting the Main Idea

Read each paragraph below. Then write what you think is the main idea of each paragraph on the lines provided.

1.   Gold fever struck thousands of people in 1848 and 1849. On January 24, 1848, gold was discovered at Sutter's Mill in California. News of the discovery soon spread all over the country. Stories about instant riches and huge gold strikes began to circulate. All across the country, "forty-niners" headed west for the gold fields of California. In their greed to find gold before it all disappeared, they left behind all their possessions. Farmers left their crops and animals. Store owners sold their shops, and factory workers quit their jobs. These victims of gold fever moved to California to stake their claims and make their fortunes.

The main idea of this paragraph is _____

_____

2.   Many different kinds of people, including outlaws, were drawn to the camps which grew up around the mines almost overnight. These camps often had no laws or government. Under these conditions, it was nearly impossible to keep law and order. Crimes were common. The stagecoaches carrying gold and silver were often robbed. As a result, citizens sometimes formed vigilante groups to bring law and order to these wild camps. The vigilantes tracked down, tried, and punished lawbreakers. By 1865, over one thousand of these unofficial police groups had been started.

The main idea of this paragraph is _____

_____

3.   Mining was important to the West because it produced great amounts of wealth and attracted many settlers. Over $2 billion in gold and silver were taken from the mines of the Rocky Mountains area by 1890. The most famous mine, the Comstock Lode of Nevada, made over $500 million between 1860 and 1880. When a new mine opened, thousands of people moved to the area. For example, the population of Virginia City, Nevada, grew by 100,000 after the nearby Comstock Lode opened. After the mines closed, many miners stayed on. Most mining camps in time became permanent towns.

The main idea of this paragraph is _____

_____

4.   By the late 1870s, most of the gold and silver near the surface had already been mined. Expensive machinery and large-scale mining methods were needed to reach the remaining deposits. Miners then began to search for other ores to mine. In 1880, it was discovered that the old Anaconda silver mine in Montana contained huge amounts of copper ore. Since electricity has just been discovered, there was a great demand for copper, which was used to make electric wire. Copper mining soon became the largest and the most valuable mining business in the western states.

The main idea of this paragraph is _____

_____

5 Railroads

Getting the Main Idea

Read each paragraph below. Choose which of the three sentences following each paragraph best states the main idea of that paragraph. Write the letter of that sentence in the blank.

_____ 1.   In the 1830s, railroads were unsafe and unpopular. Before they could become successful, several problems had to be solved. Better rails had to be developed. The iron rails then in use sometimes bent under the weight of the trains. The braking system had to be improved. The brakes could stop the engine, but all the other cars would crash into it. If the cars were stopped before the engine, they would pull back so hard that they would break away from it. The construction of bridges had to be improved to make them safer for trains. Finally, huge amounts of money were needed to lay more railroad track.

   A.   Several problems had to be solved to make railroads popular.

   B.   Railroads have always been a popular form of transportation.

   C.   Many people wanted to invest in the railroads.

_____ 2.   The railroad companies that built the transcontinental railroads received money from many different sources. The United States government gave the railroad companies a total of over $700 million. The railroads received $16,000, $32,000, or $48,000 per mile, depending on the terrain. The government also gave the railroads public land along the sides of the tracks equal to the size of the state of Texas. For every mile (1.6 kilometers) of track laid, the railroad received about ten square miles (16 kilometers) of free land. State and city governments all over the country invested in the railroads. Europeans also invested heavily. English investors alone loaned over $2.5 billion to American railroad companies.

   A.   The money for building transcontinental railroads came from many sources.

   B.   Only the United States government invested money in the railroads.

   C.   Foreigners were not allowed to invest in American railroads.

_____ 3.   The railroads helped open the West to settlement. People found it faster and safer to go west by way of train instead of by horse and wagon. The railroads also made it easier for western settlers to ship their products to the eastern cities and to receive manufactured goods back from the East. Some railroad companies encouraged people to settle along their tracks. James Hill of the Great Northern Railroad attracted settlers with offers of cheap tools, cattle, and farm machinery. Hill also helped new towns along his company's tracks build new schools and churches.

   A.   Railroad owners were interested only in making large profits.

   B.   Railroads helped open the West to settlement.

   C.   Railroad companies would not let people settle along the tracks.

_____ 4.   In the late 1800s, some railroad companies were engaged in unfair business practices that were very harmful to western farmers. Several railroads serving the same region would sometimes agree to set high prices and overcharge their customers. Rates charged by the railroads varied greatly between different parts of the country. Western farmers paid rates up to three times as high as farmers in the Midwest and East. Many railroads charged farmers a higher price for shipping goods a short distance than for a long distance. Railroads also gave rebates, or kickbacks. In other words, they refunded part of the shipping charge to their best customers. Therefore, the rate for small farmers in the West was higher than the rate for the giant eastern businesses.

   A.   Farmers are always complaining about something.

   B.   Railroads treated all their customers equally.

   C.   Some railroads unfairly charged western farmers.

6 Moving West

Learning the Vocabulary

Read each sentence below. Then complete the sentence by filling in the spaces correctly. Each dash represents one letter in the correct spelling of the word.

1. In 1848, gold was discovered at _ _ _ _ _ _ _ _ _ _ _ in California.

2. The wagon train known as the _ _ _ _ _ _ _ _ _ _ _ was trapped by snow in a mountain
   pass on the way to California. Many of the pioneers starved or froze to death.

3. The _ _ _ _ _ _ _ _ _ _ _ _ of Nevada was the most famous mine in the West.

4. During the _ _ _ _ _ _ _ _ _ _ _ _ _ _ _ _ of 1889, many people rushed to stake a
   claim on part of the Indian Territory.

5. The _ _ _ _ _ _ _ _ _ _ were people who tried to enforce law and order in the rough mining camps.

6. _ _ _ _ _ _ _ _ _ _ _ _ became the leader of the Church of Jesus Christ of Latter-Day
   Saints in 1844 after Joseph Smith was murdered by a mob.

7. _ _ _ _ _ _ _ _ _ was the owner of the Great Northern Railroad. He encouraged people
   to settle on the property along his railroad tracks.

8. A religious group, the _ _ _ _ _ _ _ , settled in Utah in the 1840s after being driven out of
   Nauvoo, Illinois.

9. _ _ _ _ _ _ _ _ _ _ was a famous mountain man and guide. He helped explore the Rocky
   Mountains.

10. In 1862, Congress passed the _ _ _ _ _ _ _ _ _ _ _ . This bill gave a farm of 160 acres
    (64.8 hectares) free to anyone willing to settle on the land and work it for five years.

7 Cowboys and Indians

Learning the Vocabulary

Unscramble the words in capital letters in each sentence. Write your answers in the blanks at the bottom of the page.

1. George Custer and all his soldiers were wiped out at the **ALTETB FO HTE TILELT IBGRHNO** by the Sioux and Cheyenne Indians.

2. **ANT OLEV** was the most famous black cowboy of the American West.

3. **EPOSJH IDEDGNL** was an Illinois farmer who patented barbed wire in 1874.

4. The **FUFALBO** were an important source of food, clothing, and shelter for the Indians.

5. **LIAWLMI DYOC,** nicknamed "Buffalo Bill," killed over five thousand buffalo in only eighteen months.

6. The **HOLMSCHI RAITL** was used to move Texas longhorn cattle north between Texas and Abilene, Kansas.

7. A **ANERREOITVS** is land set aside by the United States government as a home for Indian tribes.

8. The **ENPO NGAER** was the unfenced pasture land where the cattle of the area grazed.

9. The Indians thought the **SHOGT NCAED** would bring back to life their dead Indian friends and the herds of dead buffalo.

10. The invention of the **VOLERRVE** gave the cowboys the edge over the Indians in weapons.

1. _____   6. _____

2. _____   7. _____

3. _____   8. _____

4. _____   9. _____

5. _____   10. _____

8   The Old West

Learning the Vocabulary

The following words have been used in the main idea section. See if you can find these words in the word search puzzle below. Circle the words. They may be found vertically or horizontally. They may also overlap.

Nat Love	William Cody
Chisholm Trail	Sutter's Mill
Abilene, Kansas	Comstock Lode
open range	James Hill
buffalo	rebate
reservation	Mormons
George Custer	Homestead Act
Ghost Dance	Oklahoma Land Rush

```
O  K  L  A  H  O  M  A  L  A  N  D  R  U  S  H

D  O  A  P  O  O  D  O  P  A  A  T  O  C  D  S

C  P  C  H  I  S  H  O  L  M  T  R  A  I  L  T

T  E  T  L  T  P  O  S  R  T  L  V  B  S  J  G

U  N  C  M  C  Q  M  W  T  X  O  W  I  U  A  E

P  R  X  A  X  A  E  C  V  Z  V  M  L  T  M  O

O  A  Z  C  C  S  D  X  C  E  O  E  T  E  R

W  N  O  M  L  D  T  N  Z  D  C  R  N  E  S  G

X  G  W  F  M  R  E  B  A  T  E  M  E  R  H  E

R  E  S  E  R  V  A  T  I  O  N  O  K  S  I  C

C  G  H  O  S  T  D  A  N  C  E  N  A  M  L  U

S  C  B  U  F  F  A  L  O  R  S  S  N  I  L  S

C  O  M  S  T  O  C  K  L  O  D  E  S  L  P  T

T  Z  W  D  N  Q  T  O  G  F  L  M  A  L  Q  E

W  I  L  L  I  A  M  C  O  D  Y  N  S  R  N  R
```

9 Railroad Mileage, 1860–1900

Reading Maps and Graphs

One of the reasons that railroad mileage increased rapidly between 1860 and 1900 was that the United States west of the Mississippi River was being settled. Many thousands of miles of track were built in the Great American West during this period. Study the graph and answer the questions.

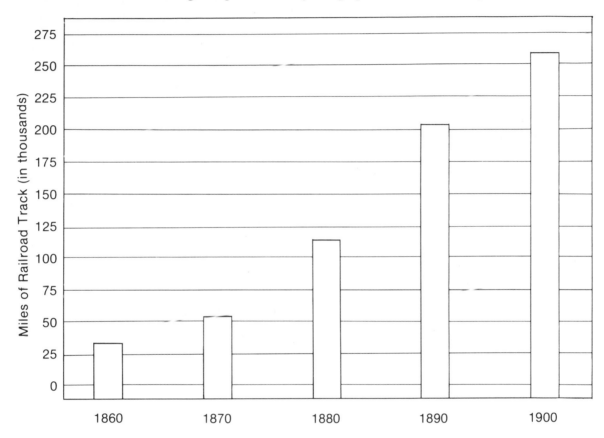

1. How many miles of track were built between 1860 and 1900? _____

_____

2. Which decade saw the biggest growth in railroad track mileage? _____

3. How many miles of railroad track were laid in that ten-year period? _____

_____

4. Which decade had the least amount of railroad construction? _____

5. How many miles of railroad track were built in that decade? _____

_____

10 Mining in the West

Reading Maps and Graphs

Mining was an important factor in causing settlers to move to the West in the latter part of the nineteenth century. Answer the questions below after studying the map.

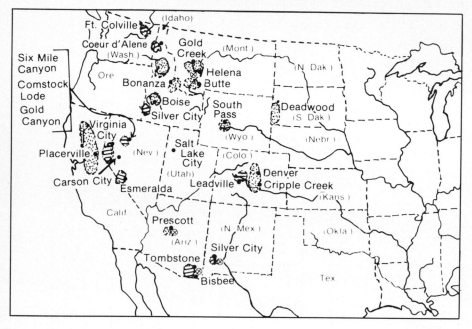

Legend:
- ▨ Gold-mining regions
- ◩ Silver-mining regions
- ⊗ Copper-mining regions

In 1860, there were only three states in the Western Territory—Texas, California, and Oregon. The names of the states that the rest of the Western Territory became are enclosed in parentheses.

1. Where was gold mined? _____

_____

2. Where was silver found? _____

_____

3. Which state or territory seems to have the most silver-mining regions? _____

4. Which states or territories mined copper? _____

5. What town is the center of the gold-mining region in South Dakota? _____

6. What *far* western states have no gold, silver, or copper? _____

7. What town is the center of the silver-mining region in Colorado? _____

8. What town is the center of the silver-mining region in Arizona? _____

9. Which state has the largest single gold-mining region? _____

10. In 1860, what type of ore appears to have been mined most extensively? _____

11 Election of 1892

Reading Maps and Graphs

As the West was being settled, the people who moved into the region became active in politics. One of the most interesting political developments during this time was the formation of the Populist party in the 1890s. The Populists were mostly people who lived in certain sections of the West and in the "Old South." They were unhappy about low farm prices, high interest rates, and what they considered to be unfair treatment by the railroads. Study the map and answer the questions.

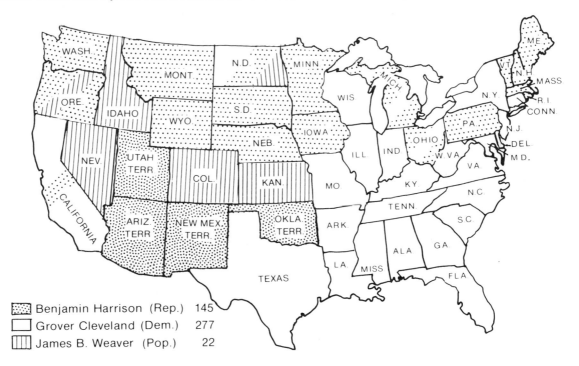

Benjamin Harrison (Rep.)   145
Grover Cleveland (Dem.)   277
James B. Weaver (Pop.)   22

1. Who was the Populist party presidential candidate in the election of 1892? _____

_____

2. How many electoral votes did the Populist candidate receive? _____

3. In which part of the United States did the Populists win electoral votes? _____

_____

4. List the states in which the Populist candidate received electoral votes. _____

_____

5. Did the Populist candidate win votes in an "old" or "new" part of the United States? _____

_____

6. Which of the three major candidates in 1892 won electoral votes in the state in which you live?

_____

12   Admission of Western States

Reading Maps and Graphs

Study the map below and then answer the questions that follow.

1.   How many western states were added to the United States in the following decades?

1810s _____   1820s _____   1830s _____   1840s _____   1850s _____   1860s _____

1870s _____   1880s _____   1890s _____   1900s _____   1910s _____

2.   How much time elapsed between the admission of the first state west of the Mississippi River and

the admission of the last state shown on the map? _____

3.   Which year saw the admission of more states than any other year? _____

4.   What states were added in that year? _____

_____

5.   How many of the states shown were added after the Civil War ended in 1865? _____

6.   Which were the last two states shown to be added to the United States? _____

_____

1 The Industrial Revolution

Getting the Main Idea

Read each paragraph below. Choose which of the three sentences following each paragraph best states the main idea of that paragraph. Write the letter of that sentence in the blank.

_____ 1.   For thousands of years, there was little change in how people made things. Skilled workers made their goods by hand, one at a time. In the 1700s, people began to experiment to find better and faster ways to make things. Complicated and powerful machines soon were developed to replace simple hand tools. A new source of power was also discovered. Steam engines began to be used to run the machines. This development of new machines and a new source of power is known as the Industrial Revolution. The Industrial Revolution greatly changed the way people lived and worked. Instead of working on goods by hand at home, people went to operate machines in factories. A whole new way of life developed.
   A. When the Industrial Revolution began, people left the factories to work at home.
   B. People have always had machines to help them.
   C. The Industrial Revolution changed the way people lived and worked.

_____ 2.   The Industrial Revolution began in England. There machines were first used to weave cloth. The English wanted to protect this advantage by making certain that other countries could not use their machines. The plans to their machines were a carefully guarded secret. The machines, their plans, and even the textile workers were not allowed to leave the country. In 1789, however, Samuel Slater, a mechanic in an English weaving mill, managed to move to the United States. Before he left, he memorized the plans of the weaving machine. In 1790, Slater built a weaving mill in Rhode Island. Samuel Slater brought the Industrial Revolution to the United States. Factories soon sprang up all over the country. Slater became known as the "father of the American factory system."
   A. Samuel Slater had a very poor memory.
   B. Samuel Slater brought the Industrial Revolution to the United States.
   C. The English were willing to share their secrets with the rest of the world.

_____ 3.   After the Civil War, factories in the United States grew very rapidly. There are several reasons for this growth. Railroads made it easy to ship raw materials to the factories and to ship finished goods across the country. New natural resources, such as coal and iron, were discovered. New sources of power, such as oil and later electricity, were found. Factories began to make new and better goods. During this time, many people from other countries moved to the United States. These immigrants provided cheap labor for the factories. Also, the population of the country grew quickly. This increased the demand for factory goods.
   A. Factories in the United States grew rapidly after the Civil War.
   B. As the population went up, factory production went down.
   C. War caused factories to produce more guns and supplies.

_____ 4.   During much of the 1800s, the United States government favored business. The government followed the theory of laissez-faire. According to this idea, government should not try to control business. Several high tariffs, or taxes on goods brought in from other countries, were passed to help American businesses. The Supreme Court often ruled in favor of business. It used the Fourteenth Amendment's equal protection clause to keep states from passing laws to check large businesses. It also ruled that unions and strikes were not legal.
   A. The Supreme Court defended the labor unions' right to strike.
   B. The government favored business during the nineteenth century.
   C. The government lowered its tariffs to please business leaders.

2   Industrial Leaders

Getting the Main Idea

Read each paragraph below. Choose which of the three sentences following each paragraph best states the main idea of that paragraph. Write the letter of that sentence in the blank.

_____ 1.   The last twenty-five years of the nineteenth century are sometimes called the Gilded Age. During this time, there was a tremendous difference between how the rich and the poor lived. The average worker earned only enough money to barely feed and clothe his family. Many people lived in dirty, crowded slum buildings without enough heat, light, or ventilation. The working conditions of many jobs were dangerous. Thousands of people were killed or injured each year. The few rich people, on the other hand, were able to spend millions just on luxuries. Cornelius Vanderbilt, for example, built a special vacation house for his family. The house itself cost several million dollars, and the Vanderbilts spent another 9 million dollars just to furnish it. Yet this house was used only seven weeks each summer.

   A. All people were treated equally in the United States.

   B. The Vanderbilt family shared their money with the poor.

   C. The rich and the poor lived very differently during the Gilded Age.

_____ 2.   Some business leaders who spent most of their lives building up their companies and their fortunes gave most of the money away when they retired. These people are known as philanthropists. John D. Rockefeller, the founder of the Standard Oil Company and the world's first billionaire, gave over $500 million to charity. He donated to churches, schools, libraries, and colleges. Andrew Carnegie, who made his millions in the steel industry, was also a famous philanthropist. After he retired, Carnegie gave away over $400 million. His money helped set up over 2,500 libraries.

   A. Philanthropists gave away their fortunes to charity.

   B. Rich men such as Rockefeller and Carnegie had no respect for money.

   C. Andrew Carnegie was the richest man in the world.

_____ 3.   J. P. Morgan was one of the greatest financiers in United States history. During the Civil War, Morgan served his country and made money for himself by selling government bonds to other countries. Morgan then began to buy up small railroad lines. The company he formed was called the Northern Securities Company. It soon controlled the country's largest railroads. Morgan twice helped the government out of financial difficulties. In 1895, a run on bank notes nearly wiped out the government's supply of gold. Morgan lent the government gold at an interest rate of only 2 percent. At the time, the standard rate was 30 percent. During the recession of 1907, Morgan bought gold for the government. When he formed the J. P. Morgan Company in 1895, Morgan was the richest person in the country. In 1901, Morgan formed the world's first billion-dollar business, the U.S. Steel Company.

   A. J. P. Morgan interfered too much in the nation's economy.

   B. J. P. Morgan became rich by cheating the government.

   C. J. P. Morgan was a great financier.

_____ 4.   When Theodore Roosevelt became President in 1905, large companies, known as trusts, controlled many industries. Roosevelt believed that the trusts had too much power for the public good. He ordered the Justice Department to break up the Northern Securities Company into smaller, competing railroads. Roosevelt also began court cases against the beef, oil, chemical, and tobacco trusts. Because he tried to break up the powerful American trusts, President Roosevelt became known as the "trust buster."

   A. President Roosevelt encouraged businesses to form trusts.

   B. Roosevelt was known as the "trust buster" because he worked to break up trusts.

   C. Theodore Roosevelt was president of the Northern Securities Company.

3 Labor Unrest

Getting the Main Idea

Read each paragraph below. Then underline the sentence that best states the main idea of each paragraph.

1. In 1900, working conditions in American factories were terrible. The workers sometimes worked fourteen hours a day. Other days, there was no work at all. Workers were paid only $15 for seventy hours of hard work. Working conditions were often very dangerous. Many workers were injured or killed while on the job. They were not paid for any injury or sickness which happened during work. Instead, they were simply fired. Factory owners sometimes owned the workers' houses and the stores where the workers shopped. They charged very high rents and prices. Workers who complained were often fired. Sometimes workers tried to organize a strike. That is, they refused to work until the owner met their demands for better working conditions and higher pay. The owners would bring in strike-breakers, known as scabs, to keep the factories open.

2. Many workers came to believe that they had to join together to protect themselves from unfair factory owners. They formed labor unions to get better working conditions and more pay. Of course, the factory owners were opposed to unions. To keep workers from joining the unions, owners used the blacklist. If they found out that any of their workers were members, owners put their names on a blacklist. Any worker on this list was fired at once. Since owners gave their blacklists to other owners, a worker on the list found it very hard to get another job. The blacklist proved to be a very effective weapon.

3. The Knights of Labor, once a powerful union, declined sharply after 1886. In 1869, the Knights of Labor had been formed to unite all workers into one national union. It invited everyone to join. Women and men, blacks and whites, immigrants and native born, skilled and unskilled were all welcome. The Knights of Labor grew very rapidly. By 1886, it had 700,000 members. By 1900, however, there were only 100,000 members. One reason for the decline was the Haymarket Riot. On May 3, 1886, workers gathered at Haymarket Square in Chicago. They were protesting the killing of several striking workers by police two days earlier. When police tried to break up the meeting, someone threw a bomb. Eleven people were killed. The Haymarket Riot turned the public against labor. Another reason for the Knights' decline was that skilled workers grew unhappy because the union took in unskilled workers. Many skilled workers left to join the American Federation of Labor, which was formed in 1886.

4. The railroad strike of 1877, the first major strike in the country, failed to win the workers' demands. The strike began when railroad workers walked off the job because of a pay cut. The railroad company hired scabs to take their place. The angry strikers tried to keep the scabs from running the trains. Battles broke out between them and the guards hired to protect the trains. The army was ordered in to stop the violence and keep the trains running. The strikers began to realize they might lose their jobs if the strike lasted much longer. They accepted the pay cut and returned to work.

5. Eugene V. Debs was an important labor and political leader for many years. In 1893, he organized the American Railway Union. By 1894, Debs had enough power to strike against the giant Northern Pacific Railroad. He won, forcing the railroad to drop its planned pay cut. In 1896, Debs led his members against the Pullman Palace Car Company of Chicago. It was the largest strike until then. Debs ordered his members across the country not to handle any train carrying a Pullman car. When Debs refused to obey an injunction, or court order, to end the strike, he was jailed for six months. While in jail, Debs became a Socialist. He ran for President as a Socialist five times—in 1900, 1904, 1908, 1912, and 1920.

4   Immigration

Getting the Main Idea

Read each paragraph below. Then write what you think is the main idea of each paragraph on the lines provided.

1.   Between 1800 and 1900, millions of people, hoping to find a better life, left their homelands and moved to the United States. Events in their own countries made these immigrants believe they should go to the United States. In some parts of the world, there were terrible food shortages. In Ireland, over a million people starved to death during the Irish potato famines of 1845 and 1846. About 1.5 million survivors moved to the United States. Other people came to the United States to escape political or religious persecution. Still others came to escape overcrowding or lack of opportunity.

The main idea of this paragraph is _____

_____

2.   For many years, people in the United States welcomed the immigrants who came here to live. These new immigrants were needed to settle the wilderness, farm the land, and work in the factories. However, by the 1880s, people began to view the immigrants as a threat. They believed that the immigrants took away jobs from American workers. The immigrants did not "fit in" with the American way of life, some said. They spoke a different language and had strange customs and clothes. Many working people wanted the United States government to pass laws restricting the number of immigrants allowed to enter the country.

The main idea of this paragraph is _____

_____

3.   Largely due to immigration, cities in the United States grew very rapidly at the end of the nineteenth century. In 1800, only six cities in the United States had a population of 8,000. By 1900, the number had grown to 448 cities. Twenty-six of them had a population of over 100,000. Between 1880 and 1900, the population of Chicago went from less than 500,000 to over 1.5 million. During the same time, the population of New York jumped from 2 million to 3.5 million. In New York City, 90 percent of the people were either immigrants or children of immigrants. In Philadelphia, one-fourth of the people were immigrants. One-third of the citizens of both Chicago and Boston were foreign born.

The main idea of this paragraph is _____

_____

4.   Jane Addams was a social worker who helped immigrants in Chicago. In 1899, she opened a settlement house known as Hull House. Addams made Hull House into a neighborhood center for immigrants. Classes were started to teach them to read and write English. Hull House also offered courses about American laws and customs. Free breakfasts for children, a day-care center for working mothers, and a free medical center were available at Hull House.

The main idea of this paragraph is _____

_____

5   Immigration and Labor Unrest

Learning the Vocabulary

Fill in the blank in each of the following sentences with the word that best fits. Use each word in the list below just once.

> railroad strike of 1877   strike
> immigrants   blacklist
> labor unions   scabs
> Knights of Labor   Jane Addams
> Hull House   Eugene V. Debs

1. To protect themselves from unfair factory owners, workers formed _____.

2. _____ , the center founded by Jane Addams, offered many activities

    for immigrants who lived in the poorest sections of Chicago.

3. A _____ is the temporary stopping of work by employees in order to force

    their employer to meet their terms for better working conditions and wages.

4. The _____ was the first major strike in the United States. Federal

    troops were called out to restore order.

5. _____ are people from other countries who have moved to the United States

    to find better jobs and better living conditions.

6. _____ helped improve the lives of many immigrants in Chicago. She had

    classes to teach them English. She also started a nursery for working mothers.

7. _____ ordered his union members not to work on trains carrying

    Pullman cars.

8. Union members who were put on an owner's _____ found it almost impossi-

    ble to get a job.

9. _____ are strikebreakers brought in to keep a factory open when the workers

    go on strike.

10. The _____ was a labor organization formed in 1869 that took in all

    workers, skilled or unskilled.

6   The Growth of Industry

Learning the Vocabulary

Match the vocabulary words on the left with the meanings on the right. Write the correct letter in the blank next to the vocabulary word.

_____ 1. tariff

_____ 2. trust

_____ 3. John D. Rockefeller

_____ 4. Samuel Slater

_____ 5. Irish potato famine

_____ 6. scabs

_____ 7. Jane Addams

_____ 8. Haymarket Riot

_____ 9. Theodore Roosevelt

_____ 10. laissez-faire

_____ 11. philanthropists

_____ 12. Northern Securities Company

_____ 13. Eugene V. Debs

_____ 14. Gilded Age

_____ 15. "trust buster"

_____ 16. J. P. Morgan

_____ 17. American Federation of Labor

_____ 18. Andrew Carnegie

_____ 19. Fourteenth Amendment

_____ 20. Industrial Revolution

A. Constitutional change that the Supreme Court used to protect American businesses

B. Bombing in Chicago that killed eleven people and turned the public against the labor movement

C. President known for breaking up trusts

D. Tax on goods coming into the United States from other countries

E. Period in the late 1800s when a few extremely wealthy Americans lived lavishly while many others were extremely poor

F. Food shortages in 1845 and 1846 that caused over a million people to starve to death because of a crop failure

G. Wealthy people who gave money to charities

H. Financier who set up the Northern Securities Company

I. Giant company that controlled a particular industry

J. The development of machines to do the work that used to be done with hand tools

K. Holding company for several railroads which President Theodore Roosevelt later broke up

L. Strikebreakers brought in to keep a factory in operation when its workers went on strike

M. Socialist candidate for President in five elections in the early 1900s

N. Founder of the Standard Oil Company and the world's first billionaire

O. Nineteenth-century theory that government should not involve itself in business affairs

P. President Theodore Roosevelt's nickname

Q. Social worker who set up Hull House to serve the people of a slum neighborhood in Chicago

R. Person who memorized the plans of the weaving machine in England and brought his knowledge to the United States

S. Union set up in 1886 that drew skilled workers away from the Knights of Labor

T. Philanthropist who helped set up over 2,500 libraries in the United States

7 Business and Labor

Learning the Vocabulary

Fill in the squares to spell out the names or terms described in the clues.

ACROSS

5. Labor union set up in 1869 that was open to all workers—women and men, blacks and whites, native born and foreign born, skilled and unskilled
7. Workers' refusal to work until their demands are met
8. Organizer of the American Railway Union who ordered his union members not to work on trains carrying Pullman cars
10. Incident in Chicago in which eleven people were killed by a bomb

DOWN

1. Founder of the Standard Oil Company who gave over $500 million to charity after he retired
2. Financier who twice helped the United States out of financial problems
3. Millionaire who made his fortune in the steel industry and became famous for giving away large sums of money
4. Wealthy man who built a special vacation house that cost several million dollars
6. English mechanic who brought the Industrial Revolution to the United States
9. Strikebreaker

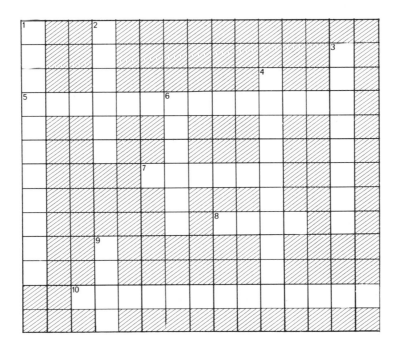

8 Industrialization Era

Learning the Vocabulary

The following words have been used in the main idea section. See if you can find these words in the word search puzzle below. Circle the words. They may be found vertically or horizontally. They may also overlap.

philanthropist	Hull House
Gilded Age	Irish potato famine
Addams	immigration
tariff	Knights of Labor
Slater	scabs
laissez-faire	labor unions
strike	blacklist
trust buster	trust

```
I  R  I  S  H  P  O  T  A  T  O  F  A  M  I  N  E
M  T  T  V  O  S  T  R  P  B  X  O  B  C  T  O  K
M  V  A  Y  R  L  V  U  C  L  A  V  L  G  C  F  N
I  A  R  A  L  A  I  S  S  E  Z  F  A  I  R  E  I
G  P  I  D  U  T  C  T  D  L  C  L  C  L  S  A  G
R  P  F  H  X  E  A  A  L  M  T  A  K  D  T  D  H
A  Q  F  K  Z  R  C  F  T  A  O  B  L  E  R  D  T
T  R  U  S  T  B  U  S  T  E  R  O  I  D  I  A  S
I  C  B  C  C  O  H  D  C  D  X  R  S  A  K  M  O
O  M  F  A  F  R  F  T  D  F  Z  U  T  G  E  S  F
N  P  I  B  H  T  Q  Q  F  G  M  N  A  E  C  N  L
T  S  M  S  J  U  R  R  G  O  N  I  F  T  T  X  A
V  V  P  H  I  L  A  N  T  H  R  O  P  I  S  T  B
L  X  S  M  L  V  J  C  D  N  T  N  A  C  D  A  O
H  U  L  L  H  O  U  S  E  L  D  S  B  T  D  F  R
```

9 Immigration, 1870–1920

Reading Maps and Graphs

The United States has been called a nation of immigrants. Since the very beginning of the country, immigrants have come to the United States from Europe, Africa, Asia, and other parts of the world. However, over the years, European immigration has been the largest and steadiest. After the Civil War, as the United States continued to industrialize at an amazingly fast pace, immigration from Europe was heavy. Notice how the immigration pattern shifted between northwestern and southeastern Europe during the time shown. After studying the graph, answer the questions below.

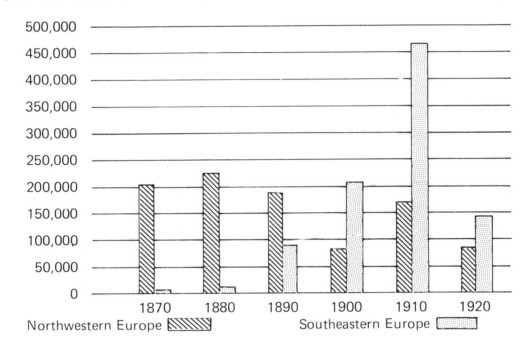

1. Before 1900, which section of Europe sent the most immigrants to the United States? _____

_____

2. In what year did southeastern Europe first surpass northwestern Europe in the number of people

who immigrated to the United States? _____

3. Which section of Europe has the smallest immigration shown? In what year? _____

_____

4. Which section of Europe had the largest immigration shown? In what year? _____

_____

5. How many southeastern Europeans immigrated to the United States in 1910? _____

10   Industrial Workers, 1870–1920

Reading Maps and Graphs

The number of workers employed in industry is a good way to tell how industrialized a country is. The graph below shows agricultural and some industrial workers. (It does not show workers in *all* industries.) Answer the questions after studying the graph.

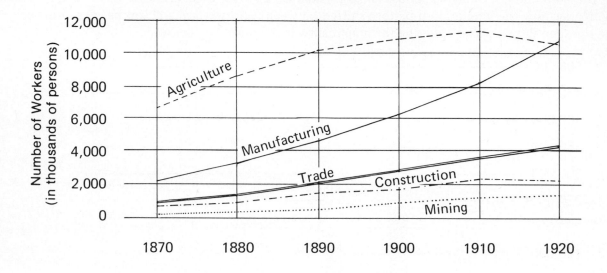

1. Did the number of workers in each of the different types of jobs shown increase between 1870 and

1920? _____

2. Which type of job shown increased most from 1870 to 1920 in number of workers? _____

_____

3. Did the number of jobs in trade increase more between 1870–1890 or between 1890–1920?

_____

4. Which type of job shown decreased the most between 1910 and 1920? _____

5. Can you conclude from the information on this graph that the United States became more indus-

trialized from 1870 to 1920? Why or why not? _____

_____

11   Steel Production, 1870–1920

Reading Maps and Graphs

Many aspects of industrial society—such as railroads, roads, machines, and buildings—require large amounts of steel. Steel production, then, is another good way of measuring how industrialized a country is. Study the line graph below and then answer the questions.

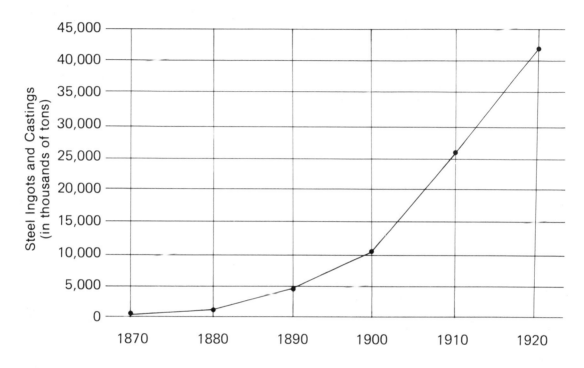

1. Did steel production increase in each decade shown on the graph? _____

2. Did the greatest increase in steel production occur before 1900 or after 1900? _____

3. Approximately how large was the increase in steel production between 1900 and 1920? _____

_____

4. Which decade saw the largest increase in steel production? _____

5. If steel production is a good way to tell how industrialized society is becoming, did the United

States become more industrialized between 1880–1890 or 1890–1900? Give your reasons. _____

_____

12   Urban-Rural Population, 1870–1920

Reading Maps and Graphs

Still another way to tell how industrialized a country has become is to compare its rural and urban populations. Generally, the more urban the population of a country, the more industrialized it has become. Study the graph and answer the questions.

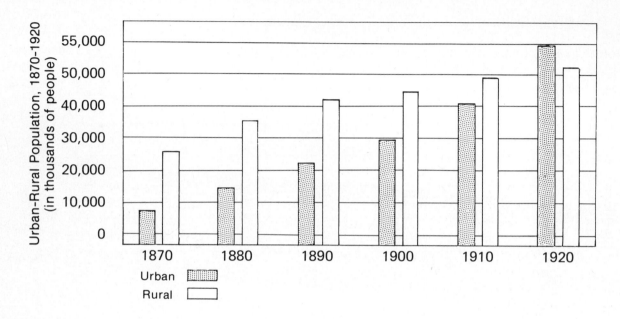

1. For most of the years shown, was the urban or rural population greater? _____

2. As you follow the graph from left to right, does the rural population seem to be gaining on the

urban, or is the urban gaining on the rural? _____

_____

3. In which year shown did the urban population surpass the rural? _____

4. Did either part of the population, rural or urban, lose people between 1870 and 1920? _____

_____

5. Was the gain in urban population from 1870 to 1900 more or less than the gain in rural population

for the same period? Give approximate figures. _____

_____

1   The Spanish-American War

Getting the Main Idea

Read each paragraph below. Then write what you think is the main idea of each paragraph on the lines provided.

1. In 1895, the Cubans rose up against Spanish rule. American newspapers, such as William Hearst's *New York Journal* and Joseph Pulitzer's *New York World*, wanted to build up their sales. They did not report the news of the revolt fairly. The "yellow press," as the newspapers were called, printed bloody and often exaggerated stories about how the Spanish tried to put down the Cubans. They never told American readers about the deaths and damage caused by the Cubans. The sensational stories of the yellow press made many Americans call for war to free Cuba.

The main idea of this paragraph is _____

_____

2. In February 1898, President William McKinley sent the U.S.S. *Maine* to the Cuban port of Havana to protect the lives and property of United States citizens from the Cuban rebels. While anchored in the Havana harbor, the *Maine* blew up and sank. Over 260 lives were lost. The sinking of the *Maine* led to the Spanish-American War. The cause of the explosion is still unknown. But many Americans blamed Spain. Whipped up by the yellow press, "Remember the Maine" became a popular call for revenge. War spirit was soon running high. Under heavy pressure, President McKinley in April 1898 asked Congress to declare war on Spain.

The main idea of this paragraph is _____

_____

3. Before the Spanish-American War began, Commodore George Dewey was secretly ordered to gather his Pacific fleet at Hong Kong to prepare for war. Dewey was further ordered to attack the Philippines, the Pacific headquarters of the Spanish navy, if war broke out. Early on May 1, 1898, Dewey sailed into Manila harbor in the Philippines and opened fire on the Spanish ships. Due to the greater range of the American guns, he was able to destroy all the Spanish ships before noon. Dewey's win in the Battle of Manila was an important victory in the Spanish-American War.

The main idea of this paragraph is _____

_____

4. In August 1898, Spain signed an armistice, or an agreement to end the fighting. In October, representatives from Spain and the United States met in Paris to work out a peace settlement. Spain agreed to grant Cuba independence and to give Puerto Rico and Guam to the United States. The United States wanted Spain to give up the Philippines too. Spain at first refused. Only after the United States offered Spain $20 million for the Philippines did Spain agree to give up the islands. The Treaty of Paris, officially ending the Spanish-American War, was signed in December 1898. The war which was begun to free one colony from Spain ended up as a war to gain overseas territories for the United States.

The main idea of this paragraph is _____

_____

2 Imperialism

Getting the Main Idea

Read each paragraph below. Choose which of the three sentences following each paragraph best states the main idea of that paragraph. Write the letter of that sentence in the blank.

_____ 1. In the late 1890s, the United States began to follow a policy of imperialism. In other words, it sought overseas colonies. It did so partly to increase its prestige as a world power. Another reason was that American business leaders wanted to gain new markets for their goods. Alaska and Midway were acquired in 1867. In 1898, the Hawaiian Islands were annexed, after American planters there led a revolt against the queen. In the same year, the United States gained Guam, Puerto Rico, and the Philippines as the result of its victory over Spain in the Spanish-American War. In 1899, Samoa and Wake Island were annexed. In 1917, the Virgin Islands were purchased from Denmark.
  A. Spain won the Spanish-American War.
  B. The United States began to acquire colonies throughout the world.
  C. The United States granted independence to the Philippines in 1898.

_____ 2. The United States wanted to build a canal across Panama, a narrow strip of land separating the Atlantic Ocean and the Caribbean Sea. A canal through Panama could cut the distance by ship between New York City and San Francisco by over half. In 1903, President Theodore Roosevelt offered Colombia, which owned Panama, $10 million in gold, plus a yearly fee, for permission to build the canal. At the last minute, Colombia turned down this offer. The people in Panama were also eager to have the canal built. Long unhappy with Colombian rule, they began a war of independence. American soldiers were sent in to keep Colombia from stopping this revolt. Panama gained its freedom and signed a treaty allowing the United States to build the canal.
  A. The Colombians were poor businessmen, since they lost the Panama Canal.
  B. The United States did not really care whether the Panama Canal was built.
  C. The United States wanted a canal through Panama so badly that it helped Panama win its independence from Colombia.

_____ 3. In a speech before Congress in 1904, President Theodore Roosevelt explained his new policy. This policy became known as the Roosevelt Corollary to the Monroe Doctrine. Roosevelt stated that the United States might have to interfere in the affairs of a Latin American country in order to keep European countries out of the Western Hemisphere. Roosevelt first used the Roosevelt Corollary to keep European countries from taking over the Dominican Republic. The Republic owed millions of dollars to European countries. These countries threatened to collect their debts by force if they were not paid at once. In 1905, the United States took over the Dominican Republic's finances. Forty-five percent of the money earned from customs was kept by the Dominican Republic. The rest went to pay the European powers.
  A. European countries always try to get things by using force.
  B. Roosevelt used his Corollary to keep Europe out of the Dominican Republic.
  C. American business leaders did not want to invest in the Dominican Republic.

_____ 4. President Theodore Roosevelt believed that a strong military was the best way to keep peace. Roosevelt thought of a plan to impress the world with the might of the United States navy. In December 1907, he ordered twenty-eight battleships, newly painted white, to sail around the world. On its voyage of 45,000 miles, this Great White Fleet impressed many countries. Japan even decided to sign a treaty with the United States that it had at one time refused.
  A. Roosevelt used the Great White Fleet to show the strength of the American navy.
  B. President Roosevelt favored the use of war to settle problems.
  C. The Great White Fleet was sent out to conquer Japan.

3 World War I

Getting the Main Idea

Read each paragraph below. Then underline the sentence that best states the main idea of each paragraph.

1. The system of alliances that divided Europe into two armed camps was a major cause of World War I. Germany, Austria-Hungary, and Italy formed the Triple Alliance. They were known later as the Central powers. Great Britain, France, and Russia formed the Triple Entente. They were known later as the Allied powers. The countries in each of these two camps promised to help one another in case of war. In 1914, the heir to the throne of Austria-Hungary was shot and killed. Austria-Hungary believed that the neighboring country of Serbia was behind the murder. Backed by Germany, Austria-Hungary made harsh demands of Serbia. The Allied powers rushed to Serbia's defense. In a few days, most of Europe was at war.

2. When World War I began, President Woodrow Wilson wanted the United States to remain neutral. Though Wilson tried to keep the country out of the war, he was finally forced into it. In 1915, a German submarine, or U-boat, sank the English liner *Lusitania.* Among the people who drowned were 128 Americans. The United States was outraged. The sinking marked a turning point in American feeling about the war. Then in 1917, the English discovered a message from the German foreign minister, Alfred Zimmerman, to the Mexican government. This note said that if war broke out between the Central powers and the United States, Mexico should attack the United States. In return, Germany promised to help Mexico gain back the land it lost to the United States during the Mexican War. The Zimmerman note angered many Americans. In April 1917, after several American ships had been sunk by German U-boats, Wilson asked Congress to declare war.

3. When the United States entered World War I in 1917, Congress gave President Wilson sweeping powers to change to wartime production. Wilson was given the power to set the price on many goods, including food. He was also given the power to take over the country's factories, mines, railroads, telephones, and telegraphs. Wilson carried out these powers through several boards or agencies. The most important one was the War Industries Board. It directed the manufacture of over thirty thousand products.

4. All fighting in World War I ended November 11, 1918, when Germany signed an armistice. The war was officially ended by the Versailles Treaty. It was signed in April 1919. Germany was severely punished by the Versailles Treaty. Germany had to give up all its colonies and all the land it had won during the war. It also had to give up some of its own land to neighboring countries. The Allies and the United States agreed to occupy the rich land west of the Rhine River in Germany. Germany was ordered to pay reparations to the Allies. These were payments for damage done by its armies. Finally, Germany was forced to admit that it was responsible for starting the war.

5. In terms of both human life and money, World War I was very costly. Over 10 million people died during the war. Another 20 million were wounded. Over 1.8 million Germans, 1.4 million French, and 1.7 million Russians were killed between 1914 and 1918. In the short time that American soldiers fought during World War I, 116,600 were killed, and 204,000 were wounded. Besides the terrible loss of life, the war was also very expensive. Property damage in Europe was over $300 billion. Fields were torn up by trenches and bombs. Whole cities were destroyed. The United States spent over $22 billion on the war and loaned another $9 billion to its allies.

4 Idealism and Isolationism

Getting the Main Idea

Read each paragraph below. Choose which of the three sentences following each paragraph best states the main idea of that paragraph. Write the letter of that sentence in the blank.

_____ 1. President Woodrow Wilson was a very idealistic man. Wilson did not want to just win the war. He wanted the war to be a "war to end all wars." He also wanted the war to "make the world safe for democracy." Before the end of the war, Wilson announced another grand plan, known as the Fourteen Points. With this plan, he hoped to prevent future wars by ending the causes of war. The plan favored such things as freedom of the seas, unrestricted world trade, and self-determination, meaning the right of all countries to rule themselves. The most important point was the fourteenth. It called for forming an organization called the League of Nations. Wilson hoped this League would keep world peace by allowing countries to settle their problems by talking instead of by fighting.

A. President Wilson was a very idealistic leader.

B. President Wilson believed that war was necessary and should be encouraged.

C. President Wilson was a very realistic and practical thinker.

_____ 2. After World War I, most Americans favored a return to isolationism. In other words, they no longer wanted the United States to take a major part in world affairs. They believed that the United States should not join the League of Nations, which was planned for in the Treaty of Versailles. Because of this, the Senate voted against accepting the Treaty in 1919. The election of 1920 also showed that most Americans did not want the United States to be a world leader. Though the Democrats did not run Wilson for President in 1920, their candidate, James M. Cox, also favored joining the League. The Republican candidate, Warren G. Harding, called for a "return to normalcy." In other words, he favored isolationism. Harding won the election easily.

A. The Senate approved the Treaty of Versailles in 1919.

B. After World War I, Americans wanted a policy of isolationism.

C. James Cox was against the League of Nations.

_____ 3. After 1919, the United States, Great Britain, and Japan tried to build up their navies. Many people wanted to stop this arms race because they feared it might lead to war. In 1921, nine powers met at Washington, D.C. At this Washington Conference, the United States, Britain, and Japan agreed to destroy some of their largest ships. They also agreed to build no more battleships and heavy cruisers for ten years.

A. At the Washington Conference, the United States announced it intended to increase the size of its navy.

B. Japan had the largest navy in the world.

C. The Washington Conference tried to keep peace by ending the naval arms race.

_____ 4. The Kellogg-Briand Pact was another attempt to end wars. The Pact outlawed war. It was written in 1928 by Secretary of State Frank Kellogg of the United States and by Foreign Minister Aristide Briand of France. Fifteen countries signed the Pact in Paris in 1928. Later, more than sixty countries signed it. All agreed to settle their problems by peaceful means. Though it had high ideals, the Kellogg-Briand Pact really had little meaning. There was no way to enforce the Pact. If a country that had signed the Pact did go to war, the other signing nations had no way to stop it.

A. The Kellogg-Briand Pact was meaningless.

B. The Kellogg-Briand Pact was able to prevent all future wars.

C. The Kellogg-Briand Pact caused World War II.

5 Becoming a World Power

Learning the Vocabulary

Unscramble the words in capital letters in each of the sentences below. Write your answers in the blanks at the bottom of the page.

1. The **MNAAPA ANCLA** cut the length of a ship voyage from San Francisco to New York City by more than half.

2. The **ATRGE TIHWE EFELT** was the name given to the twenty-eight ships that Theodore Roosevelt ordered to sail around the world in 1907.

3. American newspapers, especially a few sensational ones known as the **LWYLEO SRPES**, did not report the news of the Cuban revolt accurately. They often exaggerated stories in order to sell papers.

4. Commodore **ROGEGE EYEDW** boldly entered Manila Bay in the Philippines and defeated the Spanish fleet during the Spanish-American War.

5. President **OHROTEED ETLOEOVRS** thought that a strong military was needed to preserve peace.

6. The battleship **INMAE**, which had been sent to Cuba to protect American citizens, was sunk by an explosion.

7. Under the **ESEVOROTL OROLYRACL**, the American government would intervene in Latin American countries in order to keep European nations out.

8. The United States became involved in the **IAHSNPS-RECIMNAA AWR** in 1898 under the excuse of helping Cuba win its independence.

9. **RAIMSMIILEP** is when a country tries to conquer and rule other parts of the world.

10. **AMILWIL CMYENILK** was the President during the Spanish-American War. He sent the *Maine* to Cuba.

1. _____   6. _____

2. _____   7. _____

3. _____   8. _____

4. _____   9. _____

5. _____   10. _____

6 World War I and Its Aftermath

Learning the Vocabulary

Read each sentence below. Then complete the sentences by filling in the spaces correctly. Each dash represents one letter in the correct spelling of the word.

1. _ _ _ _ _ _ _ _ _ _ _ _ means that a country does not want to get involved with world

   affairs.

2. In May 1915, a German submarine sank the British ship _ _ _ _ _ _ _ _ _. Among the lives

   that were lost were over one hundred American citizens.

3. The _ _ _ _ _ _ _ _ _ _ _ _   _ _ _ _ outlawed war. This treaty was in time signed

   by over sixty nations.

4. President Woodrow Wilson's _ _ _ _ _ _ _ _   _ _ _ _ _ _ was a proposal for a just

   peace after World War I. President Wilson hoped it would prevent future wars.

5. The _ _ _ _ _ _   _ _   _ _ _ _ _ _ _ _ _ _, signed in April 1919, officially ended

   World War I. It was very harsh on Germany.

6. President Warren Harding's " _ _ _ _ _ _   _ _   _ _ _ _ _ _ _ _ " meant he believed

   that the United States should return to a policy of isolationism.

7. The _ _ _   _ _ _ _ _ _ _ _ _ _ _   _ _ _ _ _ was the most important wartime agency

   supervised by President Wilson. It controlled the manufacture of more than thirty thousand

   products.

8. Woodrow Wilson's Fourteen Points called for setting up the _ _ _ _ _ _   _ _

   _ _ _ _ _ _ _, the first international organization intended to prevent wars.

9. _ _ _ _ _ _ _   _ _ _ _ _ _, the President during World War I, was an idealistic leader.

10. The _ _ _ _ _ _ _ _ _ _   _ _ _ _ _ _ _ _ _ _ _ was called in 1921 to try to stop the

    naval arms race between the United States, Japan, and Great Britain.

7 The New Power

Learning the Vocabulary

The following words have been used in the main idea section. See if you can find these words in the word search puzzle below. Circle the words. They may be found vertically or horizontally. They may also overlap.

imperialism
Kellogg-Briand Pact
yellow press
Panama Canal
isolationism
Allied powers
Central powers
Dewey

League of Nations
Lusitania
World War I
Cuba
Wilson
Philippines
Roosevelt
Spanish-American War

```
K  E  L  L  O  G  G  B  R  I  A  N  D  P  A  C  T  L  P
C  P  W  C  A  V  T  C  O  M  V  P  E  L  F  D  I  U  A
E  H  O  S  L  O  C  A  O  P  P  I  W  T  E  C  S  S  N
N  I  R  T  L  B  B  J  S  E  Z  X  E  N  S  P  O  I  A
T  L  L  M  I  P  J  L  E  R  Q  D  Y  D  C  W  L  T  M
R  I  D  Q  E  D  I  O  V  I  B  W  P  O  C  U  A  A  A
A  P  W  T  D  E  L  J  E  A  L  A  T  I  O  O  T  N  C
L  P  A  V  P  T  N  A  L  L  G  A  N  B  E  S  I  I  A
P  I  R  A  O  W  S  L  T  I  Y  C  C  F  V  E  O  A  N
O  N  I  E  W  Q  U  L  V  S  P  L  N  T  G  V  N  P  A
W  E  O  T  E  X  V  I  T  M  N  D  X  B  X  D  I  F  L
E  S  L  K  R  C  Y  E  L  L  O  W  P  R  E  S  S  A  L
R  W  I  L  S  O  N  S  O  C  U  B  A  W  Z  X  M  V  X
S  L  E  A  G  U  E  O  F  N  A  T  I  O  N  S  T  G  W
W  S  P  A  N  I  S  H  A  M  E  R  I  C  A  N  W  A  R
```

8 Power Around the World

Learning the Vocabulary

Fill in the squares to spell out the names or terms described in the clues.

ACROSS

1. Document that officially ended World War I
5. Editor of the *New York Journal*, one of the "yellow press" newspapers
6. Battleship that blew up and sank in the Havana harbor
8. President of the United States during World War I
9. Name of the alliance between Germany and Austria-Hungary during World War I
10. Naval leader who defeated the Spanish fleet in the Philippines

DOWN

2. President of the United States who offered to buy Panama from Colombia
3. Name of the alliance between Great Britain, France, and Russia during World War I
4. Newspapers in the 1890s that made stories sensational in order to sell papers
7. President of the United States during the Spanish-American War

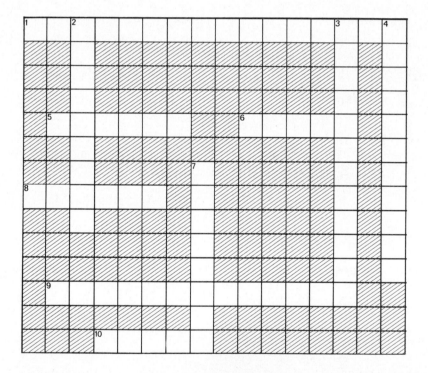

9 United States Possessions, 1903

Reading Maps and Graphs

The United States joined the international race to gain overseas colonies later than many other countries. But once it had begun the race, it moved rapidly to gain land. By 1903, the United States had extended its holdings halfway around the world. Study the map below and then answer the questions.

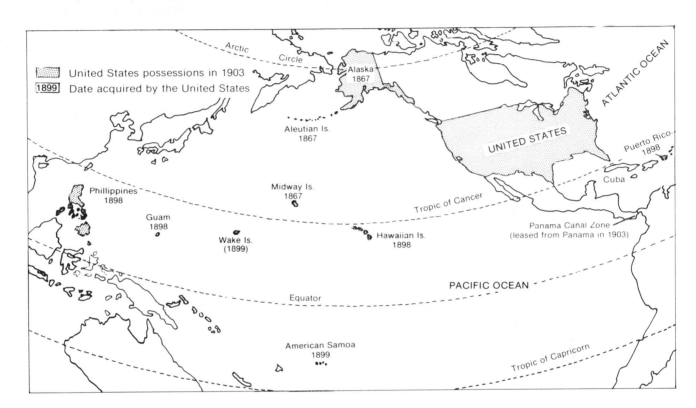

1. What United States possessions lies to the southeast of the United States? _____

2. What United States possession extends above the Arctic Circle? _____

3. In what direction from the United States are most of its other possessions? _____

4. In what ocean are these possessions located? _____

5. Name those possessions that lie in the Pacific Ocean between the Tropic of Cancer and the Tropic

of Capricorn. _____

_____

10 Foreign Trade, 1870–1920

Reading Maps and Graphs

The value of a country's exports (goods shipped out of the country) and imports (goods shipped into the country) gives a clue as to the amount of industrial and commercial activity of that nation. The amount of foreign trade, in turn, is a good indication of that country's standing as a world power. Below is a graph of import and export statistics for the United States between 1870 and 1920. Study the graph and answer the questions.

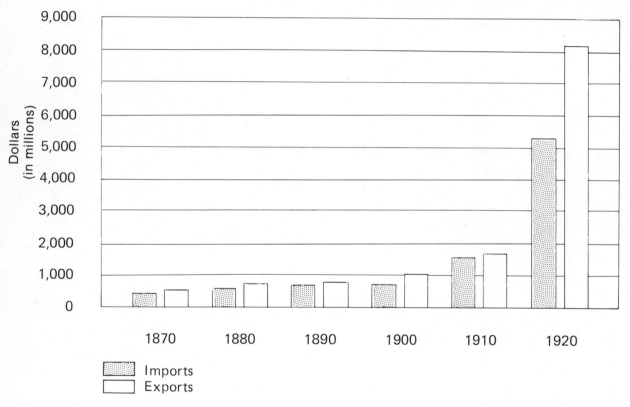

Imports
Exports

1. In which years did the value of imports exceed the value of exports? _____

_____

2. Was total trade (imports and exports added) greater in 1880 or 1890? _____

3. Did the total trade increase or decrease between 1870 and 1920? _____

4. Which ten-year period experienced the smallest increase for the time period shown? The largest?

_____

5. Which increased by the greatest amount from 1870 to 1920—imports or exports? What was the

size of the increase? _____

_____

11 World War I Alliances

Reading Maps and Graphs

For a number of reasons, Europe was divided into two opposing sides by the beginning of World War I in 1914. One country, Italy, started the war as a Central power but switched to the Allied side before the war was over. Some nations remained neutral all during the war. Eventually, the United States entered the war in April of 1917. Study the map below and then answer the questions.

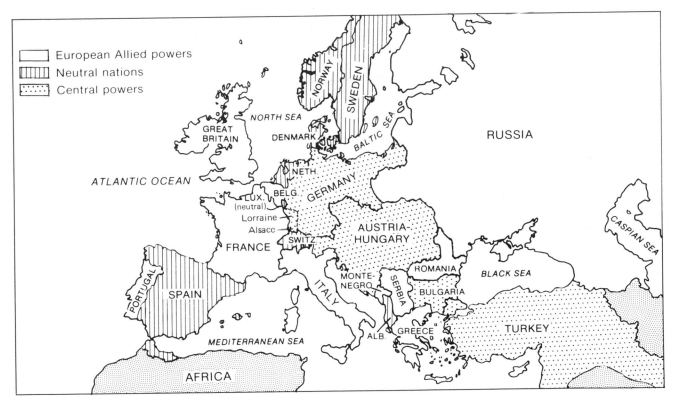

1. Which countries shown on the map belong to the Central powers? _____

_____

2. Which appears to be the largest country of the Allied powers? _____

3. To which side did Portugal belong? _____

4. List the countries that remained neutral during World War I. _____

_____

5. What Allied power is separated from the rest of Europe by water? _____

12 Europe After World War I

Reading Maps and Graphs

As a result of World War I, which ended in November 1918, the boundaries of Europe changed a great deal. Study the map below and compare it with the map on page 107. Then answer the questions that follow.

1. Alsace and Lorraine became part of France after World War I. To which country did they belong before World War I? (See page 107.) _____

2. The country of Serbia in the World War I map (page 107) is part of which new country in the after World War I map shown here? _____

3. After World War I, what countries controlled territory that Austria-Hungary controlled prior to World War I? Name two. _____

4. Did the boundaries of Switzerland change as a result of World War I? _____

5. What new nations were created after the war from parts of Germany and Russia? Name three.

_____

1 The Red Scare

Getting the Main Idea

Read each paragraph below. Choose which of the three sentences following each paragraph best states the main idea of that paragraph. Write the letter of that sentence in the blank.

_____ 1.   After World War I, the government tried to rid the country of Socialists and Communists. The years of 1919 and 1920 were known as the Red Scare. Many Americans feared that the radicals might take over the government. The Espionage Act of 1917, which had been passed during the war, was now used to jail and fine hundreds of radicals. Aliens arrested under this law were often deported, or sent out of the country, without being tried. The greatest drive took place in 1919 and 1920 under Attorney General A. Mitchell Palmer. Palmer ordered his men to jail thousands of suspected Communists and other radicals.

   A. During the Red Scare, the government tried to rid the country of radicals.
   B. Communists and Socialists took over the country in 1919.
   C. Attorney General Palmer was a Socialist.

_____ 2.   As the Red Scare died down, some citizens began to see that many people lost their rights during the Palmer raids. They pointed out that many raids had been against the law, since no search warrants had been used. Often the people jailed had nothing to do with radical groups. Some were held for weeks while the government tried to prove something against them. Others were made to sign confessions falsely stating that they were Socialists or Communists. In several cases, family members who visited the prisoners were also arrested. Though more than 6,000 people were taken in the raids, there was evidence to send only 556 out of the country.

   A. The Palmer raids did a good job of ridding the country of radicals.
   B. Almost all of those arrested in the Palmer raids were deported.
   C. The Palmer raids took away the rights of many people.

_____ 3.   Sacco and Vanzetti, two Italian immigrants, were victims of the Red Scare. In 1920, two men killed a Massachusetts paymaster. Nicola Sacco, a shoemaker, and Bartolomeo Vanzetti, a fish peddler, were jailed for this murder. Sacco and Vanzetti were good targets for those who feared aliens and radicals. They were not American citizens. Besides, they did not hide that they were anarchists. These were people who believed that all governments should be overturned. Though little could be proved, the judge believed they were guilty before the trial even began. In 1927, Sacco and Vanzetti died in the electric chair. They were put to death not because they murdered a man but because they were aliens and radicals.

   A. Sacco and Vanzetti were fairly tried and put to death.
   B. Sacco and Vanzetti were victims of the fear of foreigners and radicals.
   C. Sacco and Vanzetti arrested many foreigners during the Red Scare.

_____ 4. The feeling against foreigners led to immigration laws during the 1920s. In 1921, a quota law was passed. This law limited the number of immigrants by fixing a percentage from each country. It was aimed at southern and eastern European countries, such as Russia, Italy, and Poland. But many Americans felt that too many people were still coming from these countries. They believed that most of the radicals came from that part of Europe. An immigration act in 1924 set the quota at 2 percent of the people of each country living in the United States in 1890. This was done because most of the people from southern and eastern Europe came after 1890. In 1929, a national origins act allowed only 150,000 people to enter the country each year.

   A. Americans continued to welcome immigrants in the 1920s.
   B. Immigration was limited in the 1920s because people feared foreigners.
   C. Immigration laws in the 1920s were aimed at keeping out people from northern Europe.

2 Crime and Criminals

Getting the Main Idea

Read each paragraph below. Then write what you think is the main idea of each paragraph on the lines provided.

1.   Prohibition was a law that millions of Americans did not obey. The Eighteenth Amendment (1919) had outlawed the making, selling, or carrying of liquor. Yet people made liquor in their basements or in stills hidden in the country. Rumrunners brought it into the United States from Mexico or Canada. Speakeasies sold drinks to anyone who could say the password. At last, the government decided that prohibition had failed. In 1933, the Twenty-first Amendment ended this law.

The main idea of this paragraph is _____

_____

2.   During the 1920s, gangsters made fortunes by selling liquor. They then moved into gambling and drugs. Gangsters such as Al Capone gained great wealth and power in the 1920s. For several years, Capone really ran Chicago. He bribed police, judges, and government leaders. His army of one thousand men made daring, daytime attacks against other gangs. None of his men were ever convicted for the many murders they committed. Capone spent thousands of dollars on gifts and horse races. He even spent thousands on the funerals of other gang leaders he had ordered to be killed. He had over $6 million when he was finally jailed for not paying taxes.

The main idea of this paragraph is _____

_____

3.   In the 1920s, the Ku Klux Klan rose to great power. The Klan had been formed again in Georgia in 1915. In 1919 alone, this group lynched over seventy blacks. Its members also hated Jews, Catholics, and immigrants. In the next few years, the Klan spread to the Midwest and West. In some states, it could put people into office or cause their defeat. In 1924, the Klan moved into national politics. It blocked the nomination of Al Smith for President. Smith was a Catholic, and his parents had been immigrants. When Smith did run for President in 1928, the Klan helped to defeat him.

The main idea of this paragraph is _____

_____

4.   During his term as President (1921-1923), Warren G. Harding picked many friends for high government posts. Some of Harding's friends took part in government scandals. Harding's attorney general used his power to protect friends who broke prohibition laws. Another man cheated the government by taking a bribe during a land sale. Still another friend took nearly $200 million from the government agency he directed. The worst scandal centered on Secretary of the Interior Albert Fall. Fall was bribed to lease government oil fields at Elk Hills in California and Teapot Dome in Montana to oil companies. These deeds did not become public until Harding's term was over. Then most of the men were tried and sent to jail.

The main idea of this paragraph is _____

_____

3   Changes in American Life

Getting the Main Idea

Read each paragraph below. Then underline the sentence that best states the main idea of each paragraph.

1.   For many Americans, the 1920s were a time of prosperity. Factory workers earned twice as much in 1928 as they had in 1914. Since workers were paid more, they were able to buy many new products such as radios, washing machines, vacuum cleaners, and family cars. Between 1921 and 1929, factory production doubled. Businesses showed healthy profits. Some companies even began paying for their workers' insurance and pensions.

2.   The automobile caused great changes in the United States. Because Henry Ford's use of the assembly line and mass production made cars cheaper, more people could afford to buy them. In 1900, there were only eight thousand car owners in the United States. By 1920, there were 8 million. In eight more years, there were 26 million. By 1925, the Ford Motor Company could turn out nine thousand cars each day. Automobile production became one of the country's largest industries. As the automobile industry grew, other related industries also grew. More iron, steel, glass, rubber, and petroleum were needed. Road construction doubled between 1921 and 1929. Gas stations and roadside stands appeared in great numbers. The automobile also changed the way people lived. For example, suburbs grew as workers were able to live outside of the large cities and drive to work each day.

3.   People enjoyed new kinds of entertainment in the 1920s. Beauty contests, flagpole sitting, and dance marathons became popular. The first commercial radio station began operation in Pittsburgh in 1920. Soon millions of people across the country were listening to their favorite programs. It cost only a nickel to watch the silent movies at theaters known as nickelodeons. As many as 50 million people each week viewed these films. In 1927, audiences cheered the first sound movie, *The Jazz Singer*, starring Al Jolson.

4.   American women had greater freedom in the 1920s than ever before. For the first time, women could smoke and drink in public and be seen without a male escort. Young women shocked their mothers by wearing lipstick and bobbing their hair. Women wore their skirts shorter and did away with heavy underskirts. New stoves, washing machines, and vacuum cleaners made housework easier. By buying baked bread and canned goods, women could spend less time preparing meals. The greatest change came when women at last won their long battle for suffrage. The Nineteenth Amendment passed in time for women to vote in 1920.

5.   The Scopes trial of 1925 became well known all over the country because it brought into the open a battle between science and religion. John Scopes was a Tennessee high school teacher who was tried for teaching his class about evolution. The state of Tennessee had passed a law that the schools could not teach any idea which was against the Bible's story of creation. This law was aimed at Charles Darwin's theory of evolution. Darwin believed that all living things had developed from lower forms. His ideas shocked fundamentalists, who believed that the Bible must be taken word for word. On the other hand, Darwin's ideas were generally accepted by scientists. When Scopes was tried, he was defended by Clarence Darrow, the country's leading lawyer. The prosecution was headed by William Jennings Bryan, a fundamentalist who had run three times for President. The high point came when Bryan took the stand as an expert on religion. Darrow's attack on Bryan showed him to be no expert on either religion or science. Though Scopes was found guilty, the trial did not turn out to be the victory the fundamentalists had expected.

4   The Red Scare and Crime

Learning the Vocabulary

Fill in the blank in each of the following sentences with the word that best fits. Use each word in the list below just once.

Red Scare   immigration
evolution   prohibition
Al Capone   Sacco and Vanzetti
Ku Klux Klan   Teapot Dome
Palmer raids   Warren Harding

1. In 1919, the Eighteenth Amendment was passed, and in 1920 _____ became

   the law of the land. This law said it was illegal to make, sell, or carry liquor.

2. _____ were accused of committing murder. They were convicted of

   this crime mainly because they were foreigners.

3. The _____ was a secret organization formed against blacks, Jews,

   Catholics, and immigrants.

4. The _____ were a series of attacks against suspected radicals. Many of these

   attacks were found to be illegal.

5. _____ was the most famous gangster of the 1920s.

6. During the _____, Americans became afraid that Communists or Socialists

   might take over the United States government.

7. The _____ laws set quotas on the number and types of immigrants that could

   enter the United States.

8. Many scandals took place during the administration of _____. Several

   government officials were later found guilty of their crimes.

9. A famous trial took place after John Scopes was arrested for teaching the theory of

   _____ to his high school classes.

10. The _____ scandal took place when Secretary of the Interior

    Albert Fall illegally leased government oil reserves to a few private oil companies.

5 Excitement of the 1920s

Learning the Vocabulary

Match the vocabulary words on the left with the meanings on the right. Write the correct letter in the blank next to the vocabulary word.

_____ 1. Red Scare

_____ 2. Henry Ford

_____ 3. Charles Darwin

_____ 4. Sacco and Vanzetti

_____ 5. Teapot Dome

_____ 6. Al Smith

_____ 7. alien

_____ 8. Clarence Darrow

_____ 9. Ku Klux Klan

_____ 10. Espionage Act

_____ 11. radicals

_____ 12. Twenty-first amendment

_____ 13. Palmer raids

_____ 14. Eighteenth Amendment

_____ 15. William Jennings Bryan

_____ 16. immigration laws

_____ 17. Al Capone

_____ 18. Nineteenth Amendment

_____ 19. Albert Fall

_____ 20. Scopes trial

A. Wartime law used after the war to arrest radicals

B. Most famous gangster of the 1920s

C. Period when many people feared communism and socialism

D. Court case which brought into the open the conflict over the theory of evolution

E. Term used to describe Communists, Socialists, anarchists, and other people with extreme political views

F. Scandal that found the secretary of the interior selling government oil reserves to a few private oil companies

G. Change in the Constitution which prohibited people from making, selling, or transporting liquor

H. Secret organization of people who hated blacks, Jews, Catholics, and immigrants

I. Scientist whose theory became the subject of the Scopes trial

J. Change in the Constitution which gave women the right to vote

K. Lawyer who defended John Scopes at the famous "evolution" trial

L. Series of raids led by attorney general against Communists and other radicals

M. Leader in new ideas on how to produce better and cheaper cars

N. Change in the Constitution which ended prohibition

O. Person from a foreign country who has not yet become a citizen of the United States

P. Quotas set on the number and nationalities of immigrants who could enter the United States

Q. Dishonest cabinet officer involved in a scandal over oil reserves

R. Presidential candidate whom the Ku Klux Klan helped to defeat

S. Aliens convicted of murder mainly because they were foreigners

T. Prosecutor in the famous "evolution" trial

6 People and Happenings

Learning the Vocabulary

Fill in the squares to spell out the names or terms described in the clues.

ACROSS
1. Two men convicted of murder because they were foreigners and radicals
5. Leader in new ways to produce cars faster
7. President whose officials often ended up in jail
8. Period when people were especially afraid of aliens and radicals
9. People who entered the United States from a foreign country

DOWN
1. Court case in which a high school teacher was tried for teaching the theory of evolution
2. Most famous gangster of the 1920s
3. Law used during the 1920s to jail Communists and Socialists
4. Scandal in which a cabinet member sold government oil reserves to private companies
6. Raids against the radicals in the 1920s

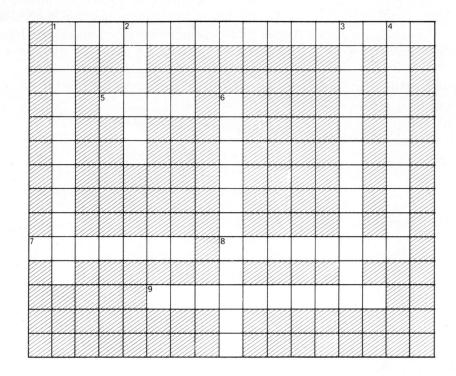

7 The Twenties

Learning the Vocabulary

The following words have been used in the main idea section. See if you can find these words in the word puzzle search below. Circle the words. They may be found vertically or horizontally. They may also overlap.

Henry Ford
suffrage
Red Scare
Espionage Act
Clarence Darrow
evolution
amendment
Al Capone

Warren Harding
Palmer raids
immigration
prohibition
Scopes trial
Teapot Dome
Ku Klux Klan
Bryan

```
N  B  I  U  I  M  M  I  G  R  A  T  I  O  N  Z  N  T
K  X  A  E  G  I  M  B  T  E  A  P  O  T  D  O  M  E
J  H  E  N  R  Y  F  O  R  D  C  Z  D  X  Q  W  C  T
F  P  S  B  Z  D  N  K  C  S  S  U  F  F  R  A  G  E
K  R  P  L  W  C  P  C  T  C  Z  Q  A  V  Y  R  P  P
U  O  I  H  R  G  Q  U  V  A  D  S  C  L  K  R  B  A
K  H  O  I  D  H  S  V  W  R  F  U  L  J  A  E  G  L
L  I  N  L  F  K  M  D  F  E  R  X  N  U  D  N  H  M
U  B  A  M  E  N  D  M  E  N  T  Z  P  R  E  H  D  E
X  I  G  E  V  O  L  U  T  I  O  N  C  I  H  A  B  R
K  T  E  R  L  P  Z  I  Q  J  L  L  W  H  L  R  I  R
L  I  A  L  C  A  P  O  N  E  C  P  Z  N  M  D  J  A
A  O  C  S  C  O  P  E  S  T  R  I  A  L  A  I  I  I
N  N  T  M  V  S  E  J  T  W  A  B  R  Y  A  N  V  D
C  L  A  R  E  N  C  E  D  A  R  R  O  W  C  G  N  S
```

8 Auto Production, 1920–1929

Reading Maps and Graphs

After World War I ended, the United States continued its rapid industrial progress. One of the most dramatic evidences of the pace of industrialization at this time is the number of passenger cars being produced. Answer the questions below after studying the graph.

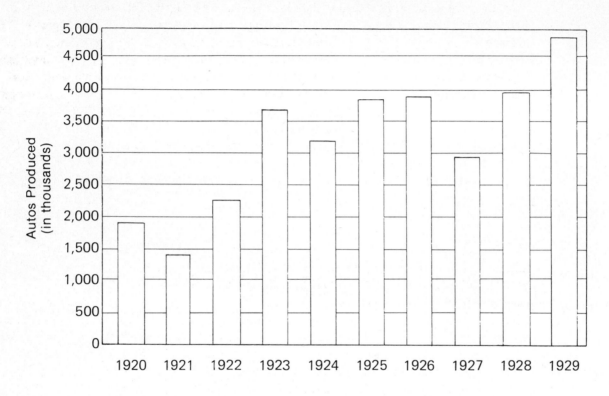

1. How many years does the graph cover? _____

2. Did auto production increase each year in the years shown on the graph? _____

3. Which years saw an increase in auto production over the previous year? _____

_____

4. Were more than twice as many cars produced in 1929 than in 1920? _____

5. What year saw the biggest increase in production over the previous year? _____

9 Airplane Production, 1920–1929

Reading Maps and Graphs

The 1920s, as you have already seen, was the decade when the automobile came into widespread use. Another form of modern transportation, the airplane, also became popular during the 1920s. While it had been used by the military during World War I, its commercial use did not develop until after the war. Study the graph below and then answer the questions.

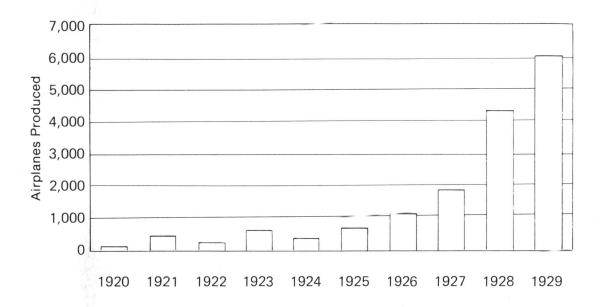

1. What years show a decrease in production? _____

2. What year experienced the greatest single increase in production? _____

3. How much did airplane production increase in that year? _____

4. How did airplane production change between the first five years of the 1920s and the last five

years? _____

_____

10   Election of 1928

Reading Maps and Graphs

The election of 1928 was noteworthy if for no other reason than that one of the two major parties nominated a Catholic as its candidate for President. Al Smith from New York was the man, and he ran as a Democrat. His opponent, Herbert Hoover, the Republican candidate, was a well-known political figure and defeated Smith rather decisively. Study the map and answer the questions.

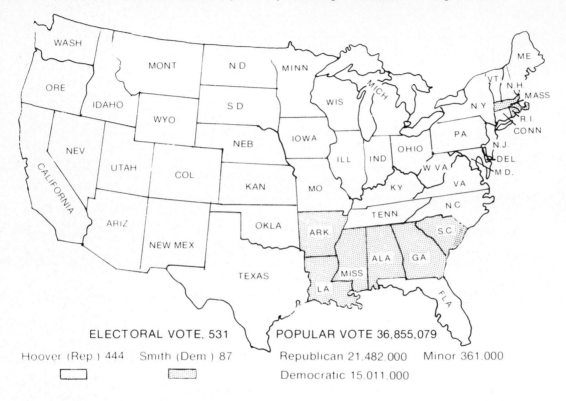

ELECTORAL VOTE, 531   POPULAR VOTE 36,855,079

Hoover (Rep.) 444   Smith (Dem.) 87   Republican 21,482,000   Minor 361,000

Democratic 15,011,000

1. How many states gave their electoral votes to Al Smith? _____

2. In which section of the country did Al Smith win the most electoral votes? _____

3. Name the states in that section of the country that voted for Al Smith. _____

_____

4. What two other states gave their electoral votes to Smith? _____

_____

5. How many more popular votes did the Republican candidate receive than the Democratic candi-

date? _____

6. Who won this presidential election in the state where you live? _____

11   Immigration, 1920–1929

Reading Maps and Graphs

European immigration into the United States had always been extensive, particularly between 1870 and 1920. However, during the 1920s, Congress passed several laws restricting immigration into the United States. Study the immigration graph below and answer the questions.

1. What year saw the largest immigration of Europeans into the United States? _____

2. What year saw the greatest drop in number of immigrants? _____

3. What year saw the second largest decrease in immigration? _____

4. Which year saw the least change in the number of immigrants? _____

   _____

5. In which five-year period did the yearly number of immigrants vary the least? _____

12 Farmers' Expenditures, 1920–1929

Reading Maps and Graphs

While some sectors of the economy prospered in the 1920s, others did not. During this period, farmers experienced financial difficulty. Increased agricultural production at home and abroad and decreased demand for American products in Europe helped to drive farm prices down. As farmers earned less, they spent less on machinery and equipment. Answer the following questions after studying the graph.

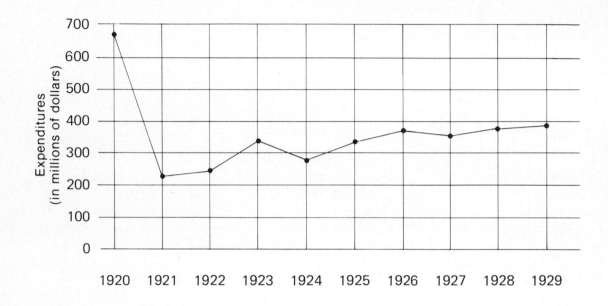

1. Which years experienced a decrease in spending for machinery and equipment compared with the

previous year? _____

2. What was the lowest year for farm spending for machinery and equipment? _____

3. After 1921, was spending rather constant, or did it vary a great deal from year to year?

_____

_____

4. Which year saw the largest increase in expenditure over the previous year? _____

5. How large was the increase? _____

1 The Great Depression

Getting the Main Idea

Read each paragraph below. Choose which of the three sentences following each paragraph best states the main idea of that paragraph. Write the letter of that sentence in the blank.

_____ 1. The stock market crash in October 1929 touched off the Great Depression. For several years before, millions of Americans had speculated, or gambled, by putting their money in the stock market. They bought a part ownership, or share, of a company at a low price, hoping to sell it later at a higher price. Many of these investments were very risky. Some people borrowed money to invest in the stock market. Others bought on the margin. This meant that they made a small down payment on the price of the stock, promising to pay the rest later. In 1929, prices rose to dangerous levels. When the stock market crashed in October, the value of stocks suddenly dropped. Investors sold their stock in panic. Nearly $30 billion was lost. Small investors lost their life savings. Millionaires lost their fortunes.

   A. The stock market crash of 1929 led to the depression.

   B. Stock prices increased when the crash occurred.

   C. Buying stock was a safe investment in 1929.

_____ 2. Between 1929 and 1939, the United States was hit by its worst depression. During those years, life was very difficult for many Americans. Thousands of banks and businesses failed. Over 12 million workers lost their jobs as factories all over the country closed. Workers lucky enough to keep their jobs had their pay cut drastically. Many families lost their life savings. Old clothes had to be repaired to last many years. Finding food became a problem. Some families hunted for scraps in garbage dumps. Others received handouts from charity. Each day, thousands waited in long bread lines for free soup and bread.

   A. During the depression, people were lazy and just wanted free handouts.

   B. Unemployment was very low during the depression.

   C. Life for many Americans was difficult during the depression.

_____ 3. During the Great Depression, many Americans lost their homes. Even in good times, few people had enough money to buy a house in cash. Most families went to a bank and took out a house loan, known as a mortgage. They then made monthly payments to repay the loan. If they were unable to make their mortgage payments, the bank would foreclose. That is, the bank would take possession of the house. When the Great Depression struck, many Americans were not able to make their payments. Driven out of their houses, people had to get along as best they could. Some moved in with friends or relatives. Others lived in shacks that sprang up in many cities.

   A. Large apartment buildings housed the homeless during the depression.

   B. During the depression, many Americans lost their homes.

   C. Most people bought their homes in cash.

_____ 4. President Herbert Hoover did not believe that the federal government should give direct aid to the victims of the Great Depression. Hoover believed in "rugged individualism." He thought that if people came to depend on the government for help, they would lose their independence. Aid to people without homes or jobs, Hoover believed, should be handled by state and city governments and charities. In 1932, he vetoed a bill to give direct aid to the poor and create jobs for those out of work. Though he would not aid private citizens, Hoover did try to help business. In 1932, he set up the Reconstruction Finance Corporation. It loaned over $2 billion to large businesses, banks, and insurance companies.

   A. Hoover believed that the government should give direct aid to depression victims.

   B. Hoover did not think the government should give people direct relief.

   C. Hoover signed a bill creating jobs for the unemployed.

2 The New Deal

Getting the Main Idea

Read each paragraph below. Choose which of the three sentences following each paragraph best states the main idea of that paragraph. Write the letter of that sentence in the blank.

_____ 1. Franklin D. Roosevelt was the Democratic candidate for President in 1932. He did not agree at all with Hoover over what the government should do about the Great Depression. Roosevelt wanted the government to help people get back on their feet again. He also believed that the government should pass laws to make sure that a depression would never happen again. During the 1932 campaign, Roosevelt promised a "new deal for the American people." He easily defeated Hoover and was sworn in as President in 1933.
   A. Roosevelt believed that depressions were inevitable.
   B. Roosevelt wanted to help the victims of the depression.
   C. Roosevelt was the Republican candidate for President in 1932.

_____ 2. President Roosevelt wanted to restore people's trust in the banks. On his first day in office, he closed all the banks in the country for four days. Roosevelt called for this "bank holiday" to stop bank runs, in which people took all their money out of the banks. Roosevelt next asked for an Emergency Banking Relief Act. This law gave him power to regulate banks and to open the banks again in good condition. Roosevelt then made a radio speech telling the country that the government stood behind the banks about to reopen. He promised people that their money was safer in a bank than under a mattress at home. The next day, the banks opened again. Many people put their money back in the banks.
   A. President Roosevelt wanted to restore people's confidence in the banks.
   B. The Emergency Banking Relief Act closed all the banks on holidays.
   C. Roosevelt believed that banks were unsafe and urged people to keep their money at home.

_____ 3. In June 1933, Roosevelt acted to bring long-lasting reform to banking. He signed the Glass-Steagall Banking Act. This law was intended to keep bankers from speculating with money deposited in their banks. In June, the Federal Deposit Insurance Corporation was set up to insure bank deposits. If a bank should ever fail, the government promised to pay bank depositors' losses up to $2,500.
   A. Roosevelt's attempts to bring long-range reform to banking were not successful.
   B. Roosevelt acted to protect the safety of bank deposits.
   C. The Federal Deposit Insurance Corporation allowed banks to speculate with bank deposits.

_____ 4. The National Recovery Administration was set up in 1933. The NRA called for business and labor leaders to set up fair practice codes. The government hoped that these rules could limit production and so raise prices. The workweek was to be cut to forty hours, and workers were to receive pay raises. This would help open up more jobs. The codes also tried to end unfair competition. Business and labor leaders agreed to set up over six hundred codes. Over 90 percent of businesses, employing over 22 million workers, were covered by these rules.
   A. Few businesses and workers were covered by the NRA codes.
   B. The NRA set fair practice codes for business and labor.
   C. The NRA codes were set up to increase production and to limit prices.

3 New Deal Programs and People

Getting the Main Idea

Read each paragraph below. Then write what you think is the main idea of each paragraph on the lines provided.

1. In 1933, the Agricultural Adjustment Administration was set up to help farmers earn more money by producing less food. Farmers were asked not to plant one-fourth to one-half of their land and to raise only half as many animals. By 1933, cotton growers agreed not to plant 10 million acres. Hog raisers agreed to kill 6 million hogs rather than send them to market. In 1934 and 1935, farmers across the country planted 30 million acres less than they had in 1932. Because the supply of farm products went down, farmers received higher prices for them. The government also gave the farmers cash for each acre they did not plant.

The main idea of this paragraph is _____

_____

2. In 1933, Roosevelt named Frances Perkins as the United States secretary of labor. Perkins became the first woman cabinet member in the country's history. Perkins played a leading part in setting up many of the New Deal's most important programs. She had the idea of the Civilian Conservation Corps. The CCC put over 2.7 million young men to work in the national forests. She also headed a group which led to the Social Security Act. This act set up an old-age pension plan. Perkins also greatly improved the Immigration Service. Government officials were sent to other countries to help prepare immigrants for their journey to the United States.

The main idea of this paragraph is _____

_____

3. The Tennessee Valley Authority was established in 1933. The TVA set out to improve life in the Tennessee Valley, which covered states drained by the Tennessee River. It built twenty-one dams to control flooding. Power plants were built to provide electricity to the people at low cost. Trees were planted to end soil erosion. Acres of land were made into parks for the people to enjoy. The TVA also drew industry to the area.

The main idea of this paragraph is _____

4. Harry Hopkins created jobs for millions of people out of work during the Great Depression. In 1933, Roosevelt made Hopkins head of the Federal Emergency Relief Administration. Thousands of families received money for food, clothes, and housing through the FERA. But Hopkins believed that the unemployed needed jobs, not free handouts. He wanted to put people back to work as soon as possible. When an aide came up with a plan which would work in the long run, Hopkins answered, "People don't eat in the long run." In 1935, Roosevelt put Hopkins in charge of the Works Progress Administration. The WPA built roads, bridges, schools, and hospitals. As head of this program, Hopkins found jobs for 8.5 million workers at a cost of $11 billion.

The main idea of this paragraph is _____

_____

4 Criticism of the New Deal

Getting the Main Idea

Read each paragraph below. Then write what you think is the main idea of each paragraph on the lines provided.

1. President Roosevelt's New Deal programs were criticized by some people in the United States. Some Americans believed that the programs were too costly. Under the New Deal, they argued, the government was spending more than it received in taxes. They noted that the national debt had doubled between 1929 and 1934. Other Americans charged that the New Deal gave the government too much power. They felt that the government was moving into areas where it did not belong. They feared that Roosevelt was headed toward socialism. They were especially against the Tennessee Valley Authority. They believed that the TVA was driving private power companies out of business.

The main idea of the paragraph is _____

_____

2. Senator Huey P. Long of Louisiana offered his "Share Our Wealth" plan as an alternative to the New Deal. Long, also known as the "Kingfish," believed that Roosevelt was not doing enough to help people suffering from the depression. Long wanted to place a limit of $1 million on the amount of money any person could have. The government would take anything over that amount. With all the money taken from the rich, Long planned to help the poor. He promised to give every family a car, a radio, and a $6,000 house. He also called for a free pension and free college education.

The main idea of this paragraph is _____

_____

3. Charles E. Coughlin, a Catholic priest, was very much against Roosevelt's New Deal. Father Coughlin spoke on a weekly religious radio broadcast which reached millions of Americans. The "radio priest" received more mail than anyone else in the country, including Roosevelt himself. Coughlin had no clear political program. But each week his attacks against Roosevelt became sharper. He once called Roosevelt the "dumbest man ever to occupy the White House."

The main idea of this paragraph is _____

_____

4. In 1936, Alfred M. Landon of Kansas ran for President on the Republican ticket. Landon did not attack most of the New Deal programs. He promised only to balance the budget and to return some powers to the states. In his campaign, Roosevelt pointed out the success of the New Deal. Industrial production and national income were up, and unemployment was down. When the vote came in, Roosevelt carried every state but two. He received 27.7 million votes to Landon's 16.6 million. Roosevelt's strong victory showed that the American people were still in favor of the New Deal.

The main idea of this paragraph is _____

_____

5 Names and Terms of the 1930s

Learning the Vocabulary

Match the vocabulary words on the left with the meanings on the right. Write the correct letter in the blank next to the vocabulary word.

_____ 1. Federal Emergency Relief Administration

_____ 2. Herbert Hoover

_____ 3. "radio priest"

_____ 4. "Share Our Wealth" plan

_____ 5. Federal Deposit Insurance Corporation

_____ 6. New Deal

_____ 7. "Kingfish"

_____ 8. Emergency Banking Relief Act

_____ 9. Works Progress Administration

_____ 10. Tennessee Valley Authority

_____ 11. Reconstruction Finance Corporation

_____ 12. Agricultural Adjustment Administration

_____ 13. Franklin D. Roosevelt

_____ 14. Civilian Conservation Corps

_____ 15. Alfred M. Landon

_____ 16. Huey P. Long

_____ 17. National Recovery Administration

_____ 18. Frances Perkins

_____ 19. Great Depression

_____ 20. Charles E. Coughlin

A. Huey Long's nickname

B. Secretary of labor who was the first woman cabinet member

C. Government agency that helped farmers earn more money by producing less

D. Government agency that provided thousands of families with food, clothing, and shelter during the depression

E. Republican party's candidate for President of the United States in 1936 who carried only two states

F. Government agency which guarantees to pay back people's deposits if the bank fails

G. President of the United States who thought up the New Deal

H. Government agency that improved life in parts of seven states by building dams and electric plants

I. President when the Great Depression began

J. Catholic priest who attacked President Roosevelt on his weekly radio programs

K. Government agency which created jobs for the unemployed by having them build schools, hospitals, roads, and bridges

L. Period of hard times which began with the stock market crash in 1929

M. Senator from Louisiana who was very critical of President Roosevelt

N. Government agency that loaned money to businesses during the depression

O. Father Charles E. Coughlin's nickname

P. Government agency that put young men to work in the national forests during the depression

Q. Law which gave Roosevelt power to regulate banks in order to restore people's trust

R. Huey Long's plan to take money from the wealthy and give it to the poor

S. President Franklin D. Roosevelt's program to end the Great Depression

T. Government agency that called for fair practice codes for business and labor

6 The Great Depression

Learning the Vocabulary

Read each sentence below. Then complete the sentence by filling in the spaces correctly. Each dash represents one letter in the correct spelling of the word.

1. In the 1920s, many people speculated by putting their money in the _ _ _ _ _

    _ _ _ _ _ _.

2. A certificate that shows a person has a part ownership in a company is called a _ _ _ _ _.

3. Some people would make a small down payment on the price of stock and promise to pay the

    rest later. This is called buying on the _ _ _ _ _ _.

4. Unsafe investments led to the stock market _ _ _ _ _ in October 1929.

5. Many people in the United States lost their homes as well as their jobs during the

    _ _ _ _ _ _ _ _ _ _.

6. A bank loan on a house is called a _ _ _ _ _ _ _ _.

7. If a family could not make monthly payments on their house loan during the depression, the

    bank would _ _ _ _ _ _ _ _ _, taking possession of the house.

8. _ _ _ _ _ _ _ _ _ _ _ _ was President of the United States when the Great Depression

    began. He did not believe it was the federal government's responsibility to give direct aid to the

    people.

9. The _ _ _ _ _ _ _ was Franklin D. Roosevelt's program to help the victims of the Great

    Depression.

10. _ _ _ _ _ _ _ _ _ _ _ _ _ _ _ _ was elected President of the United States in 1932.

7 The Depression Years

Learning the Vocabulary

Fill in the squares to spell out the names or terms described in the clues.

ACROSS
2. Presidential candidate who in 1932 promised Americans a "new deal"
7. Loan from a bank to buy a house
8. Head of the FERA in 1933 and the WPA in 1935 who created millions of jobs for unemployed workers during the depression
9. Period of time starting in 1929 when many people were unemployed

DOWN
1. What many people unwisely put their money into during the 1920s
2. First woman to serve in a presidential cabinet
3. Roosevelt's program to help people through the depression
4. Term for gambling on the stock market
5. Event in 1929 that marked the beginning of the Great Depression
6. President when the depression began

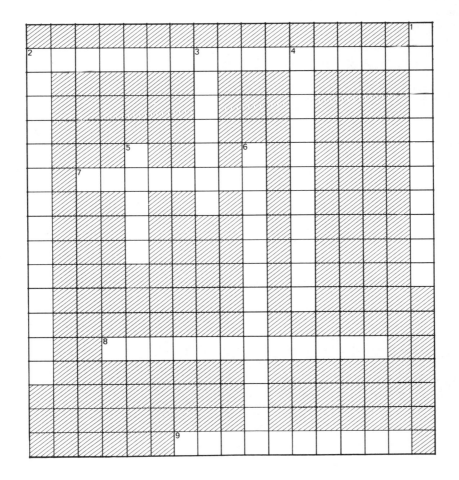

8 Puzzling Out the 1930s

Learning the Vocabulary

The following words have been used in the main idea section. See if you can find these words in the word search puzzle below. Circle the words. They may be found vertically or horizontally. They may also overlap.

radio priest	Father Coughlin
bank holiday	Kingfish
Share the Wealth plan	Franklin Roosevelt
Harry Hopkins	speculation
stock market	Alfred Landon
socialism	Herbert Hoover
crash	New Deal
Huey Long	national debt

```
S  H  A  R  E  T  H  E  W  E  A  L  T  H  P  L  A  N
O  N  L  I  C  P  U  C  R  A  S  H  O  E  G  I  C  H
C  A  F  A  T  H  E  R  C  O  U  G  H  L  I  N  F  E
I  T  R  S  B  S  Y  C  X  A  F  I  A  G  R  S  J  R
A  I  E  T  A  U  L  T  D  O  V  C  R  D  A  P  L  B
L  O  D  O  N  W  O  I  C  B  Z  Q  R  F  D  E  O  E
I  N  L  C  K  I  N  G  F  I  S  H  Y  L  I  C  P  R
S  A  A  K  H  Z  G  N  R  S  A  C  H  N  O  U  G  T
M  L  N  M  O  L  A  E  P  Q  O  S  O  Q  P  L  V  H
B  D  D  A  L  D  M  W  C  B  X  T  P  T  R  A  Z  O
F  E  O  R  I  Q  O  D  T  C  V  W  K  V  I  T  Q  O
I  B  N  K  D  Z  C  E  A  C  D  M  I  X  E  I  C  V
E  T  A  E  A  X  E  A  C  L  O  N  N  Y  S  O  A  E
Q  F  D  T  Y  B  T  L  I  M  H  R  S  B  T  N  C  R
F  R  A  N  K  L  I  N  R  O  O  S  E  V  E  L  T  B
```

9   Unemployment Rate, 1930–1939

Reading Maps and Graphs

A depression is a time when prices are usually low, unemployment is high, and business activity is very slow. In the 1930s, the people of the United States experienced the worst depression in the history of the country. Study the line graph below and answer the questions.

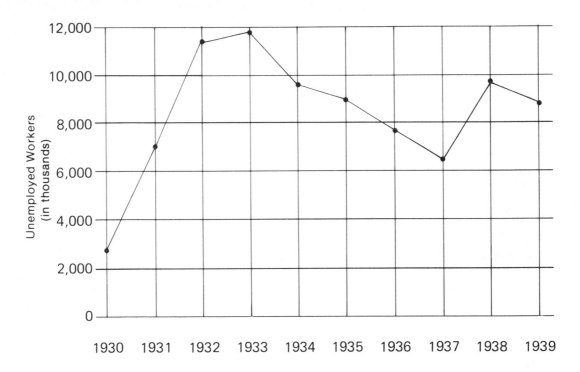

1. In which two years was unemployment the highest? _____

2. In which year did unemployment reach its greatest total? _____

3. Unemployment decreased every year after 1933 with the exception of one year. Which year was

that? _____

4. Was unemployment higher in 1939 or in 1930? _____

5. What was the difference in unemployment between 1939 and 1930? _____

_____

10 Business Activity, 1929–1939

Reading Maps and Graphs

A good method for determining the level of business activity is to look at the number of manufacturing establishments and the value of what they produce. When more firms are operating and the value of their products is higher, this usually shows greater business activity. Fewer firms and lower value mean less business activity. Study the chart below and answer the questions.

	NUMBER OF ESTABLISHMENTS	VALUE OF PRODUCTS
1929	206,663	$67,994,041,000
1931	171,450	$39,829,888,000
1933	139,325	$30,557,328,000
1935	167,916	$44,993,699,000
1937	166,794	$60,712,872,000
1939	184,230	$56,843,025,000

1. In which year did the value of manufactured products reach its lowest level? _____

2. In which year did the number of establishments reach its lowest level? _____

3. Was the value of products in 1939 more or less than the value of products in 1929? By how much?

_____

4. Which year appears to have experienced the greatest business activity? Why did you pick that

year? _____

_____

5. How would you describe what happened to the number of establishments between 1929 and

1939? _____

_____

_____

11 Income and Expenditures, 1930–1939

Reading Maps and Graphs

As the depression developed in the 1930s, the federal government began spending more money than it received in taxes. This practice is known as deficit spending. Deficit spending was used because its supporters thought that government spending would help create jobs for the unemployed. Study the graph on federal income and expenditures and then answer the questions.

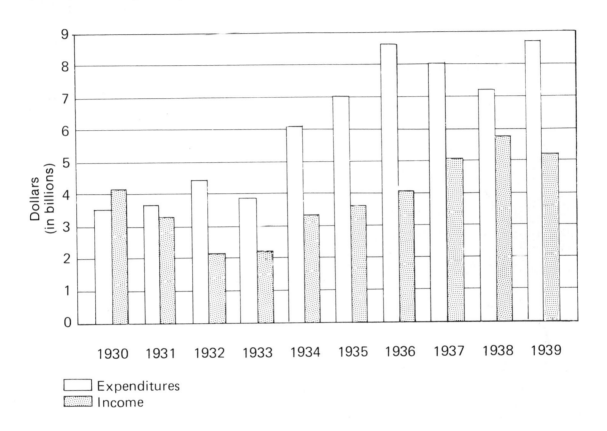

Expenditures
Income

1. In only one year during the 1930s did government income exceed expenses. Which year was that?

_____

2. In which year was deficit spending the greatest? What was the amount of the deficit that year?

_____

3. After 1933, which year had the least amount of deficit spending? What was the amount of the

deficit that year? _____

4. In which two years did the government have the smallest yearly income? _____

5. In which three years did the government spend the most money? _____

12   National Income, 1930–1939

Reading Maps and Graphs

National income is a good indicator of how prosperous the people of a nation are in any given year. National income is the total income that the people of a nation earn in a year. The income can be in the form of wages, interest, profits, or rent. Study the graph below and answer the questions.

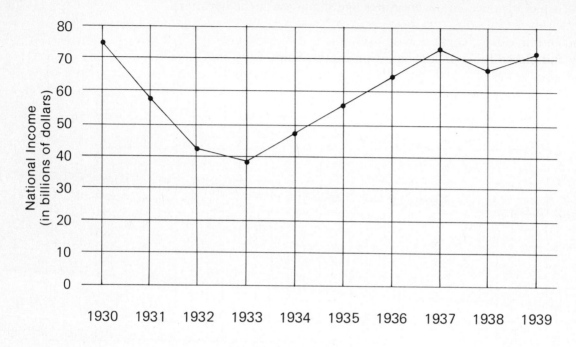

1. In which years during the 1930s did national income decrease? _____

2. From the information on this graph, in which year do you think the most people were suffering

   the most financially? Why? _____

   _____

3. In which year did national income begin to increase? _____

4. Was national income in 1939 higher or lower than it was in 1930? _____

5. What was the difference in national income between 1939 and 1930? _____

   _____

1 World War II

Getting the Main Idea

Read each paragraph below. Then underline the sentence that best states the main idea of each paragraph.

1. When Adolf Hitler became Germany's leader in 1933, he set out to destroy the Jews. Hitler and the members of his Nazi party believed that Germans were a master race. They thought that Jews, Slavs, and certain other people were inferior and had to be wiped out. Hitler rounded up Jews all over Germany and placed them in concentration camps. Some were used for slave labor. Others were tortured and killed. During World War II, Hitler's attack against the Jews spread. Jews from defeated European countries were murdered by the millions. By the end of the war in 1945, over 6 million Jews had been killed. Several million non-Jews had also been killed.

2. On Sunday morning, December 7, 1941, Japan made a surprise attack against the United States bases at Pearl Harbor, Hawaii. This two-hour attack was the worst military disaster in the country's history. Nineteen American ships were either sunk or badly damaged, crippling the Pacific fleet. Over 160 planes were destroyed before they could take off. More than two thousand Americans were killed, and another two thousand were wounded. The attack on Pearl Harbor shocked the country and quickly led to war with Japan. President Franklin Roosevelt stated that December 7 would live as a "day of infamy." On December 8, Congress declared war on Japan. Three days later, Germany and Italy declared war on the United States.

3. Fear about the loyalty of Japanese Americans led to a terrible injustice during World War II. Some Americans thought that Japan might attack the west coast and that Japanese Americans might help Japan. Over 110,000 Japanese Americans were placed in relocation camps until the war ended. They were treated as prisoners. They lived in rough barracks, fenced in by barbed wire and guarded by soldiers. The Japanese Americans protested this treatment. Yet, the Supreme Court ruled in 1944 that this measure was legal in time of war. It was not until later that the country came to understand how terribly the Japanese Americans had suffered. In 1989, the U.S. Congress passed a bill authorizing a $20,000 payment to each person who had been placed in a relocation camp.

4. On D-Day, June 6, 1944, American and British troops led by General Dwight D. Eisenhower crossed the English Channel to attack German-held land in France. The D-Day invasion was the largest attack by air, land, and sea in history. During the night of June 5, over one hundred huge gliders and over nine hundred planes left airfields in Great Britain. They dropped thousands of soldiers by parachute behind the German lines in France. As dawn came, planes dropped thousands of tons of bombs on the German defenses. Shortly after, four thousand ships landed over 120,000 soldiers along a sixty-mile beach on the French coast. Two weeks later, 1 million more soldiers had arrived. By the end of the next month, another million men, 500,000 extra vehicles, and millions of tons of weapons and supplies had landed.

5. In July 1945, the United States demanded that Japan surrender or be destroyed. Japan did not believe this warning and went on fighting. Harry S Truman, who had become President after the death of Franklin Roosevelt, then ordered that a newly developed atomic bomb be used against Japan. Truman believed the bomb might shock Japan into ending the war. On August 6, 1945, a single American plane dropped the world's first atomic bomb on the city of Hiroshima. With the power of over twenty thousand tons of dynamite, this new weapon was terribly destructive. Over eighty thousand people were killed. Most buildings inside a four-mile radius were destroyed. Thousands of people became ill or died from the radiation. Another bomb was dropped on Nagasaki four days later. The following day, Japan finally surrendered and World War II ended.

2 The Cold War

Getting the Main Idea

Read each paragraph below. Then write what you think is the main idea of each on the lines provided.

1.   After World War II, the United States and Russia competed with one another for world power. This struggle for power became known as the Cold War. During the Cold War, the United States wanted to contain, or halt the spread of, Russian communism. In 1947, when Greece and Turkey seemed about to fall to communism, President Truman sent them $400 million in military aid. This plan was known as the Truman Doctrine. In western Europe, the United States acted quickly to repair war damages and to create jobs so that the people there would not be drawn to communism. Under the Marshall Plan, $12 billion in aid was given to western European countries.

The main idea of this paragraph is _____

_____

2.   During the Cold War, Senator Joseph R. McCarthy of Wisconsin led a search for Communists inside the government. His attacks became known as McCarthyism. McCarthy made many reckless charges that he could not prove. In a well-known speech, McCarthy stated that he knew the names of 207 Communists in government. The next day, he said there were really only 57. Teachers, authors, labor leaders, and others who found fault with the government were called Communists. McCarthy even charged President Truman with being "soft" on Communists.

The main idea of this paragraph is _____

_____

3.   After World War II, Korea was divided into two separate countries. North Korea sided with Russia. It set up a Communist government. A democratic government, friendly to the United States, was formed in South Korea. Both governments claimed to rule all of Korea. In 1950, North Korea, later joined by Communist China, attacked South Korea. The United States quickly sent in soldiers to help South Korea. After nearly three years of war, a truce was signed. The border between North and South Korea was drawn at the 38th parallel. For more than three decades, Korea has remained divided. U.S. troops are stationed in South Korea to aid in its defense.

The main idea of this paragraph is _____

_____

4.   Fidel Castro, a Communist revolutionary, took over the government of Cuba in 1959. The United States did not like a Communist government in Cuba and tried to overthrow Castro. It began to work secretly with a group of Cubans who had escaped to the United States after Castro took power. These men wanted to invade Cuba. President John F. Kennedy approved plans to give them training, transportation to Cuba, and air and naval backing. In April 1961, about 1,200 of the exiles landed in Cuba at a place known as the Bay of Pigs. The invasion was poorly planned, and at the last minute, Kennedy did not authorize the necessary air support. As a result, three days later most of the invading force was killed or captured.

The main idea of this paragraph is _____

_____

3 The 1950s

Getting the Main Idea

Read each paragraph below. Choose which of the three sentences following each paragraph best states the main idea of that paragraph. Then write the letter of that sentence in the blank.

_____ 1.   For many years, students in the South attended segregated schools. That is, blacks and whites went to separate schools. In 1954, in the case of Brown vs. the Board of Education of Topeka, Kansas, the Supreme Court ruled that segregation was not legal. Many southern states did not like the court's order. They believed that the government had no right to tell them what to do with their schools. They refused to obey the order. Some states even said that they would do away with their public schools rather than allow blacks and whites to attend the same schools. In Arkansas, the governor refused to allow blacks to attend the all-white Little Rock Central High School. The President had to order federal troops into Arkansas and other southern states to see that the court's desegregation order was obeyed.
    A. The southern states quickly obeyed the order to end school segregation.
    B. The President of the United States favored segregated schools.
    C. The southern states did not like the Supreme Court order to end school segregation.

_____ 2.   In the fall of 1955, President Dwight D. Eisenhower had a dangerous heart attack. His illness caused people to worry over who was in charge of the country. Vice-President Richard M. Nixon governed the country while Eisenhower gained back his health. But the Constitution did not say who should govern if a President was not able to do his job. To take care of this, the Twenty-fifth Amendment was passed in 1967. This amendment calls for the Vice-President to take over the country if the President dies, resigns, or becomes disabled.
    A. Vice-President Nixon used the Twenty-fifth Amendment to govern the country.
    B. President Eisenhower's illness focused attention on the office of Vice-President.
    C. Vice-President Nixon refused to lead the nation when President Eisenhower was ill.

_____ 3.   During the 1950s, the United States and Canada worked closely together to build the St. Lawrence Seaway. These two countries had long dreamed of making the St. Lawrence River wider and deeper. This would allow ocean-going ships to sail from the Atlantic Ocean to the interiors of both countries. In 1953, President Eisenhower agreed to the building of locks, canals, and power plants along the St. Lawrence River. A channel was dug between Montreal and Lake Ontario, and locks were built. A commission made up of Canadians and Americans worked together to plan the construction. It decided how the electric power generated by the Seaway would be shared. It also set up shipping rates. In 1959, the billion-dollar Seaway was finished.
    A. The United States and Canada worked together on the St. Lawrence Seaway.
    B. The St. Lawrence Seaway was built and used only by the United States.
    C. President Eisenhower blocked construction of the St. Lawrence Seaway.

_____ 4.   The two states that joined the Union in 1959 were valuable additions. Alaska is rich in wood, furs, fish, gold and other minerals, and oil and natural gas. Alaska is also important for military reasons. The Distant Early Warning (DEW) line is located there. DEW is a radar system which can warn of attacks by Russian planes or missiles. Hawaii, the fiftieth state, is a group of eight large and many small islands. It is located 2,400 miles southwest of San Francisco. Hawaii is a stop-over point for ships and planes headed for Asia. Important naval and air bases are built there. Hawaii also grows millions of dollars worth of sugar and pineapples each year.
    A. The Distant Early Warning line is located in Hawaii.
    B. Alaska and Hawaii were valuable additions to the United States.
    C. Alaska is made up of a series of islands.

4 The 1960s

Getting the Main Idea

Read each paragraph below. Choose which of the three sentences following each paragraph best states the main idea of that paragraph. Write the letter of that sentence in the blank.

_____ 1. In October 1957, Russia launched the world's first satellite, called *Sputnik*, into orbit around the earth. Many Americans worried because the Russians were far ahead of the United States in their space program. The United States entered a space race against Russia. The Americans soon began to catch up. In 1961, President John F. Kennedy set the goal of safely landing a man on the moon by 1970. This goal was reached eight years and $36 billion later. On July 20, 1969, Neil Armstrong stepped out of his Apollo 11 spacecraft onto the moon's surface. Though the Russians had an early lead, the United States won the space race.

A. Russia won the space race in October 1957 with *Sputnik*.

B. The United States put the first man into space.

C. Although the Russians had an early lead, the United States won the space race.

_____ 2. The Peace Corps was set up by President Kennedy in 1961 to promote peace and friendship by sending American volunteers to help developing countries. These volunteers were mostly young men and women of college age. After receiving training, they were sent to countries in Africa, Asia, or South America. There, they worked and lived with the people. They built schools, taught nutrition, or helped farmers learn better ways to farm. By 1970, over ten thousand people were serving in the Peace Corps in sixty different countries.

A. The purpose of the Peace Corps was to promote peace and friendship by sending volunteers to developing countries.

B. The Peace Corps was a great failure since few countries asked for help.

C. Sixty countries sent Peace Corps volunteers to the United States.

_____ 3. The 1960s were a violent decade. Riots broke out in many of the large cities, such as Newark, Detroit, and New York. The worst riot took place in Watts, a black neighborhood in Los Angeles, in 1965. The riot lasted for six days. Thirty-four people were killed, 850 were wounded, and 3,100 were arrested. Over $200 million in property was destroyed. The violence of the 1960s was also clear in the number of assassinations. Several of the country's leaders were senselessly killed. President John F. Kennedy was shot and killed during a parade in Dallas, Texas, in 1963. Dr. Martin Luther King, Jr., the civil rights leader and winner of the Nobel Peace Prize, was killed in Memphis, Tennessee, in 1968. Also in 1968, John Kennedy's brother, Robert F. Kennedy, was killed in Los Angeles while campaigning for President.

A. The cities and college campuses were peaceful throughout the 1960s.

B. The decade of the 1960s was a time of violence.

C. Troublemakers got what they deserved in the 1960s.

_____ 4. Vice-President Lyndon B. Johnson became President after John Kennedy was killed. Johnson wanted to build the "Great Society." He started a number of programs to make the United States a better place to live. When Johnson signed the Economic Opportunity Act in 1964, he declared a "war on poverty." This act created jobs and set aside money for job training for poor people. Johnson's Civil Rights Act of 1964 outlawed racial discrimination in job hiring. It also outlawed segregation in public places and schools. The Medicare program in 1968 helped people over sixty-five with the rising costs of hospital care.

A. President Johnson did little to end poverty and discrimination.

B. President Johnson approved of school segregation.

C. Johnson's Great Society tried to make the United States a better place to live.

5   The Vietnam War and Its Background

Getting the Main Idea

Read each paragraph below. Then underline the sentence that best states the main idea of each paragraph.

1.   Following the Japanese surrender in 1945, the Vietnamese national leader, Ho Chi Minh, hoped to restore independence to his nation. President Harry Truman, seeking French cooperation in the setting up of the North Atlantic Treaty Organization, accepted France's determination to regain control over its colony Vietnam. The United States began to support France with money and supplies, but not with troops. When France faced defeat in 1954 at Dien Bien Phu, President Dwight Eisenhower refused to aid France militarily. Later that year the Geneva Accords were signed, temporarily dividing Vietnam along the 17th parallel until free elections could be held in 1956. The elections were never held. Communist guerrillas, called Viet Cong, began opposing the government of South Vietnam. In response, Eisenhower increased the number of U.S. military advisers in South Vietnam to 685. By early 1961, a full-scale war was being fought in Vietnam. The new President, John Kennedy, sent another 800 military advisers to help train the South Vietnamese army.

2.   By 1964, President Lyndon Johnson had increased the number of U.S. advisers in Vietnam to 23,000. He believed that more military force was needed to convince North Vietnam to give up its plan to defeat the South Vietnamese forces and unify the country under communist rule. He intended to bomb North Vietnam. Following a North Vietnamese naval advance against U.S. ships in the Gulf of Tonkin, the U.S. Congress passed the Gulf of Tonkin Resolution. At the time, Johnson did not tell the Congress that the attacked U.S. ships were actually supporting a South Vietnamese attack on the North by means of intelligence operations. The Tonkin Resolution gave Johnson the power he wanted to resist communist attacks from the North. Johnson used this power to send American soldiers to Vietnam in ever-increasing numbers. By the end of 1965, more than 125,000 American soldiers were fighting in Vietnam. U.S. involvement in Vietnam kept growing. Johnson now ordered the bombing of targets in North Vietnam. By 1968, the number of U.S. troops in Vietnam had grown to 540,000.

3.   In the late 1960s, the United States was sharply divided over the Vietnam War. One group, known as "doves," believed that the war was a terrible mistake. They wanted U.S. soldiers pulled out of Vietnam. Some young men escaped the draft by moving out of the country. Others burned their draft cards or deserted because they felt that the war was wrong. The doves charged that the war was illegal, since Congress had never declared war. Another group, known as "hawks," wanted the United States to stay in Vietnam. They believed that increased military activity would result in a victory for U.S. troops defending an ally against communist aggression.

4.   In January 1968, North Vietnamese forces launched the Tet Offensive, overrunning many villages and cities in South Vietnam, and even threatening the U.S. embassy in Saigon. Although this offensive was repulsed with heavy losses to the attackers, the effect on both public opinion and government planning in the United Sates was profound. For the first time the war began to be seen as "unwinnable." In March, Johnson halted the bombing of North Vietnam, asked Ho Chi Minh to discuss peace negotiations, and withdrew himself from the approaching presidential campaign.

5.   After a bitter presidential campaign in 1968, Richard Nixon was elected President. He quickly announced a plan for ending the war in Vietnam. His plan was to "Vietnamize" the war, returning major responsibility to the government of South Vietnam. U.S. troops were to be slowly but steadily withdrawn. Popular opinion against the continuing war grew even stronger, however. Huge public demonstrations took place, even in Washington, D.C. Nixon secretly expanded the war into neighboring Cambodia in order to deny North Vietnamese troops a safe sanctuary. This action caused renewed public protests and demonstrations against the war. Nixon continued slow withdrawal of troops. He also resumed bombing of North Vietnam, in order to pressure the regime to seek peace. By early 1972, a peace settlement was arranged, and all American forces were brought home from Vietnam. Nearly 58,000 Americans had died in the Vietnam War.

5   The 1970s

Getting the Main Idea

Read each paragraph below. Then underline the sentence that best states the main idea of each paragraph.

1.   In 1972, President Richard Nixon and Vice-President Spiro Agnew were reelected by the largest margin in United States history. Yet, within two years both Agnew and Nixon had to resign. In October 1973, Agnew became the first Vice-President in history to resign. He did so after it was discovered that he had accepted bribes while he was governor of Maryland. Nixon then appointed Gerald R. Ford as his Vice-President. In August 1974, Nixon became the first President to resign, because of Watergate charges. Nixon had tried to cover up, with the aid of his White House staff, the fact that there had been an authorized burglary of the Democratic Party National Committee's offices in the Watergate building. This bizarre act was carried out for the stated purpose of preventing leaks of confidential information from government sources. Nixon professed to know nothing about the break-in. Journalistic and later Congressional investigations revealed that responsibility for the burglary and the subsequent coverup attempt lay in the White House. When forced to release his taped conversations about the Watergate coverup, Nixon became convinced that he faced impeachment and conviction if he did not resign. Ford then became President. In turn, Ford chose Nelson Rockefeller as his Vice-President. For the first time in history, the men serving as President and Vice-president were appointed rather than elected.

2.   In 1978, a Democrat from Georgia was elected President of the United States. Jimmy Carter was his name. Carter's term as President was characterized by both successes and failures. He had campaigned as a common, down-home person. He said he knew what it was like to be an ordinary citizen. However, he lacked knowledge about the way the federal government worked. Although a Democrat, he was unable to gain the cooperation of a Democratic Congress. The rate of inflation continued to be high, and no government policies were successful in reducing it. In foreign affairs, Carter enjoyed some triumphs. He was able to negotiate a treaty with Panama, approved by the U.S. Senate in 1978. By the terms of this treaty, control over the Panama Canal will revert to Panama at the end of 1999. In the always-tense Middle East conflict, Carter was able to work out a peace treaty between Israel and Egypt. This agreement was known as the Camp David Accords. Carter's main failure was that he was unable to solve the Iranian hostage problem. Fifty-two United States citizens were held prisoner by Iranian revolutionaries in the U.S. Embassy in Teheran for many months. Carter could not get the hostages released. A military rescue was attempted, but failed. The hostages were set free on the day after Carter left office.

3.   By 1980, President Carter had become unpopular. People still liked him as a person but thought he was not a very strong leader. The Democrats, however, chose him as their candidate in 1980. Usually a President in office will be re-elected. Carter did not campaign very much. He said he was busy with his job as President. The Republicans chose Ronald Reagan as their candidate. People knew of him because he had been a movie star. He also had been a successful governor of California. His pleasant personality made him a popular candidate. However, some people were concerned because he was almost 70 years old at the time of the election. Reagan promised that if he won the federal government would reduce taxes and improve the economy. On election day with only 51 percent of voters going to the polls, Ronald Reagan proved to be the more successful candidate and was elected President.

7 Politics After World War II

Learning the Vocabulary

Unscramble the words in capital letters in each of the sentences below. Write your answers in the blanks at the bottom of the page.

1. One section of the **TNYTEW - TFFIH** Amendment says if the President is removed from office, dies, or resigns, the Vice-President becomes President.

2. In 1954, the Supreme Court ruled that **RGATESGENOI** of schools was not legal.

3. An event that caused President Carter's popularity to decrease was when Iranians took over the United States Embassy in Iran and kept the people inside it as **SEGATHOS**.

4. **WROBN** vs. the **RDOBA FO ATUDIEOCN** was the United States Supreme Court decision that outlawed racial discrimination in public schools.

5. The **ICEDAMER** program calls for the government to pay for hospital and medical care for old people.

6. The United States and Canada worked together to build the **TS CWNEERAL YASWAE**.

7. The **IILCV HIRTSG TAC** prohibited discrimination in employment and outlawed segregation in schools and public places.

8. **AIIWAH** was the fiftieth state to join the Union.

9. The United States became deeply involved in the **TVEIMNA** War between 1961 and 1968.

10. The launching of **KIPTUNS** led to the space race between Russia and the United States.

1. _____   6. _____

2. _____   7. _____

3. _____   8. _____

4. _____   9. _____

5. _____   10. _____

8   Names of the Era

Learning the Vocabulary

Fill in the squares to spell out the names described in the clues.

ACROSS
1. General who led the D-Day invasion and later became President of the United States
4. President of the United States after Richard Nixon resigned
5. Vice-President of the United States who resigned after being accused of taking bribes while governor of Maryland
8. Leader of Germany during World War II
9. President of the United States who ordered the dropping of the first atomic bomb
10. President who was the founder of the "Great Society"

DOWN
2. President who was forced to resign because of Watergate
3. President when World War II began
6. First man to walk on the moon
7. United States senator from Wisconsin who accused President Truman of being "soft" on Communists

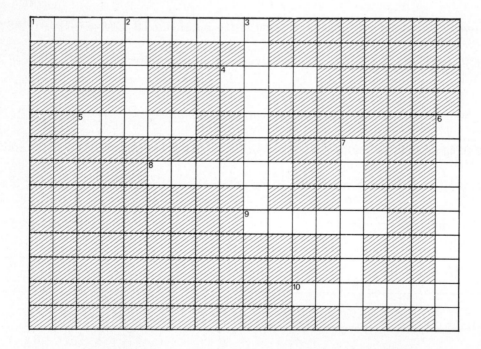

9 The 1940s and 1950s

Learning the Vocabulary

The following words have been used in the main idea section. See if you can find these words in the word search puzzle below. Circle the words. They may be found vertically or horizontally. They may also overlap.

containment	Pearl Harbor
Adolf Hitler	Harry Truman
Marshall Plan	Dwight Eisenhower
relocation camp	communism
D-Day	atomic bomb
Cold War	Nazi
Hiroshima	Fidel Castro
Nagasaki	McCarthyism

```
D  W  I  G  H  T  E  I  S  E  N  H  O  W  E  R
D  F  G  D  A  C  O  L  D  W  A  R  A  C  C  D
A  I  E  M  C  O  S  C  C  C  Z  C  D  R  E  A
Y  D  K  C  S  N  R  F  T  T  I  D  B  P  T  T
C  E  A  C  F  T  G  J  V  V  O  P  T  E  C  O
F  L  D  A  H  A  R  R  Y  T  R  U  M  A  N  M
J  C  O  R  I  I  G  E  I  A  V  B  N  R  C  I
L  A  L  T  R  N  H  K  A  E  W  G  A  L  O  C
P  S  F  H  O  M  K  L  C  G  Y  J  G  H  M  B
T  T  H  Y  S  E  M  P  F  J  T  P  A  A  M  O
V  R  I  I  H  N  O  Q  G  K  U  R  S  R  U  M
Z  O  T  S  I  T  Q  U  H  M  W  S  A  B  N  B
A  P  L  M  M  D  S  W  L  P  I  W  K  O  I  H
D  Q  E  O  A  P  T  Z  M  S  C  X  I  R  S  I
M  A  R  S  H  A  L  L  P  L  A  N  C  O  M  L
R  E  L  O  C  A  T  I  O  N  C  A  M  P  B  R
```

10 The 1960s and 1970s

Learning the Vocabulary

The following words have been used in the main idea section. See if you can find these words in the word search puzzle below. Circle the words. They may be found vertically or horizontally. They may also overlap.

segregation	Richard Nixon
doves	Great Society
Watts riot	Spiro Agnew
hawks	Medicare
Martin Luther King	Civil Rights Act
Watergate	Lyndon Johnson
Neil Armstrong	Gerald Ford
John Kennedy	Peace Corps

```
M  A  R  T  I  N  L  U  T  H  E  R  K  I  N  G

A  C  Z  L  P  C  S  X  H  A  C  S  P  A  E  R

Z  F  P  Q  H  A  E  B  I  W  T  P  J  G  I  E

F  H  B  M  J  V  G  C  L  K  P  I  O  F  L  A

H  I  A  E  M  D  O  V  E  S  B  R  H  D  A  T

L  Y  N  D  O  N  J  O  H  N  S  O  N  I  R  S

I  L  C  I  U  Z  J  Z  M  C  C  A  K  J  M  O

K  P  P  C  W  O  T  P  P  B  D  G  E  W  S  C

M  Q  W  A  T  E  R  G  A  T  E  N  N  A  T  I

P  U  U  R  X  A  L  A  Q  T  A  E  N  T  R  E

Q  X  C  E  Z  C  O  C  U  C  V  W  E  T  O  T

P  E  A  C  E  C  O  R  P  S  Q  C  D  S  N  Y

S  E  G  R  E  G  A  T  I  O  N  U  Y  R  G  B

G  E  R  A  L  D  F  O  R  D  T  W  U  I  L  E

W  A  T  R  I  C  H  A  R  D  N  I  X  O  N  L

C  I  V  I  L  R  I  G  H  T  S  A  C  T  C  H
```

11 Europe After World War II

Reading Maps and Graphs

Europe experienced some territorial changes after World War II. It also soon became divided between pro-Western and pro-Communist nations. Compare the map below with the map of Europe after World War I on page 108. Then answer the following questions.

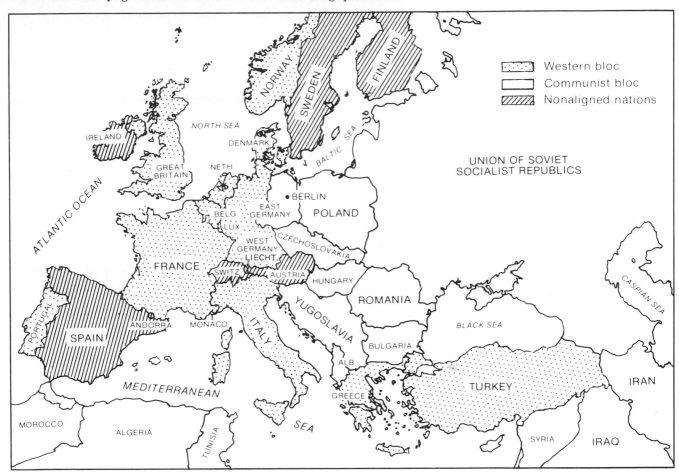

1. What has happened to Estonia, Latvia, and Lithuania? _____

_____

2. What has happened to Germany? _____

3. Berlin had long been the capital of Germany. Where is it located now? _____

_____

4. What countries are nonaligned or neutral? _____

_____

5. What two Western bloc countries are not located in western Europe? _____

12   National Debt, 1960–1990

Reading Maps and Graphs

One of the characteristics of United States government finance since the 1930s has been deficit spending. While the nation has had a debt during most of the years of its history, the debt has grown especially since the 1930s. World War II, the Korean War, the Vietnam War, and inflation account for much of the current debt. Study the graph below, left and then answer the questions below, right.

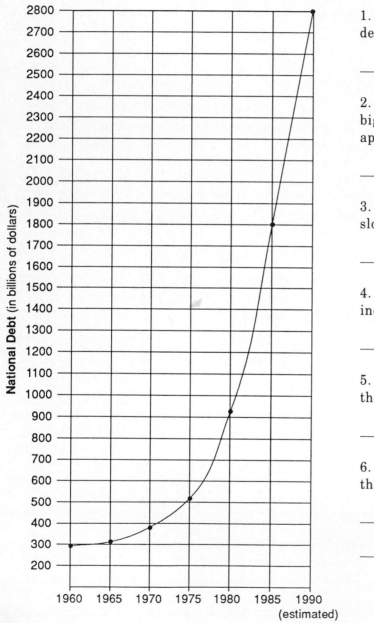

1. In which five-year period did the national debt increase the least?

_____

2. Which five-year period experienced the biggest increase in the debt? What was the approximate amount of the increase?

_____

3. From 1960 to 1970, did the debt increase slowly, or was the increase relatively large?

_____

4. What has been the approximate dollar increase in debt from 1960 to 1990?

_____

5. How much did the debt increase during the five-year period in which you were born?

_____

6. What generalization can you make about the U.S. national debt from 1960 to 1990?

_____

_____

1 The Changing World

Getting the Main Idea

Read each paragraph below. Choose which of the three sentences following each paragraph best states the main idea of that paragraph. Write the letter of that sentence in the blank.

_____ 1. American astronauts have explored the lunar landscape. The U.S. space program, however, has given the world more than just men on the moon. Many discoveries made in the program have improved the lives of millions. Radio, television, and telephone beams are bounced off satellites, making world-wide communication easier. Pictures sent to earth have helped find schools of fish in the ocean, minerals under the ground, and diseased trees in a forest. Satellites are also used to learn about the weather. With the space age have come great advances in medicine. Much has been learned about the human body because of tests done on astronauts. Transistors, computers, and freeze-dried foods have been discovered or improved because of the space age.

A. American astronauts were the first space travelers to explore the moon's surface.

B. Discoveries made by the space program have benefited millions.

C. The future of the U.S. space program is secure.

_____ 2. An energy crisis developed in 1973 when the Arab members of OPEC temporarily stopped shipping oil to the United States. This oil embargo was in response to United States support of Israel during the Yom Kippur War. Car manufacturers in the United States then began to build smaller cars that got better gas mileage. By the mid-1980s, OPEC was no longer able to maintain the high price of oil, since their share of the world market had declined. Oil thus became cheaper, and consumption again began to increase. Although car makers kept working toward better gas mileage for their engines, the average size of cars again began to increase. Overall, the energy crisis continues today because total supplies of oil are finite and eventually will be completely used up. Alternative sources of energy are being investigated, including solar energy, wind energy, and controlled nuclear fusion, among others. Many experts felt that conservation of energy continues to be of great importance in the short term while scientists investigate additional sources of energy.

A. Car manufacturers produced larger cars during the Arab oil embargo.

B. The design of American cars changed because of the energy crisis.

C. Most Americans do not believe an energy crisis exists.

_____ 3. Scientists agree that the millions of tons of pollutants being poured into the air are changing the earth's temperature, but they are not certain how. Some scientists feel this will lead to a greenhouse effect. They believe that the heat from the sun will be trapped on the earth's surface by pollution instead of bouncing back into space. If this is true, the world's temperature will rise. Giant icebergs will melt, raising the sea level and flooding the lands along the coasts. Other scientists do not agree. They think that pollution will have a quite different effect. They believe that the clouds of pollution will keep the heat of the sun from reaching the earth's surface. If this is true, the earth's temperature will fall. This might lead to another Ice Age.

A. Scientists agree that the world's temperature is dropping.

B. Scientists do not agree on how air pollution will affect the world's climate.

C. The greenhouse effect predicts the coming of another Ice Age.

_____ 4. In April, 1989, a massive oil spill took place near the port of Valdez on the Alaskan coast. A supertanker, the *Exxon Valdez*, grounded on a reef that tore open its bottom, spewing millions of gallons of crude petroleum directly into the water. Exxon and Coast Guard efforts to limit the effects of the spill were first delayed and then hastily put into motion. As the oil spread quickly, polluting the water both on and below the surface, wildlife of many kinds were affected. The spill gravely damaged the fishing industry, a mainstay of the local economy. To combat the effects of the spill, hundreds of workers were brought to the area by Exxon. As the worst of many bad oil spills that took place worldwide during the 1970s and 1980s, the *Exxon Valdez* disaster highlighted the risks of transporting petroleum in giant tankers.

A. The *Exxon Valdez* disaster took place in the 1970s.

B. Alaska outlawed the shipping of petroleum in supertankers.

C. The *Exxon Valdez* oil spill showed the risks of shipping petroleum in supertankers.

2 The News in Review

Getting the Main Idea

Read each paragraph below. Choose which of the three sentences following each paragraph best states the main idea of that paragraph. Write the letter of that sentence in the blank.

_____ 1.   January 20, 1981, was a day for celebration throughout the United States. Many voters were happy to see Ronald Reagan inaugurated as the fortieth President. Many more citizens—no matter what their political preferences—were happy to see 52 Americans set free. The 52 had been held hostage in Iran for 444 days. On January 25 the U.S. Air Force jet carrying the former captives landed on American soil. Buses took them to temporary rooms at West Point, New York. Some 20,000 people lined the bus route to welcome their fellow countrymen back home.

A. President Ronald Reagan was inaugurated on January 20, 1981.

B. The Iranian hostage crisis ended on January 20, 1981.

C. A presidential inauguration and an end to a hostage crisis made January 20, 1981, a happy day for Americans.

_____ 2.   President Ronald Reagan won re-election in a landslide victory on November 6, 1984. He carried 49 states. His opponent, former Vice-President Walter Mondale, carried only his home state of Minnesota and the District of Columbia. Reagan received 525 electoral votes, more than any previous presidential candidate. The sweeping victory apparently reflected voter approval of the nation's strong economic recovery and the administration's military build-up plans.

A. In the 1984 presidential election, Ronald Reagan received a record number of popular votes.

B. Walter Mondale lost the election because of his ties with the unpopular Carter administration.

C. President Ronald Reagan easily won reelection in 1984.

_____ 3.   In 1987, President Reagan and Soviet leader Mikhail Gorbachev met together for the third time. At this meeting they reached agreement on a treaty that bound each nation to get rid of all its intermediate-range nuclear missiles. This was the first major step toward arms reduction taken by the superpowers since the Strategic Arms Limitation Talks (SALT) treaties of the 1970s. President Reagan continued to support plans to develop and deploy a system of missile defenses known as the Strategic Defense Initiative, or "Star Wars."

A. Reagan and Gorbachev agreed to reduce nuclear missiles.

B. The SALT treaties of the 1970s were cancelled.

C. Gorbachev resigned from office in 1987.

_____ 4.   George Bush, Ronald Reagan's Vice President for eight years, won the nomination for President at the Republican Convention in 1988. Michael Dukakis became the Democratic candidate. Bush overcame an early Dukakis lead in the sample polls taken during the year and easily won the election in November. Bush ran on a platform similar to that of Reagan, and emphasized his determination not to raise taxes. Bush also stated his intention to follow a policy of watchfulness toward the Soviet Union and Soviet leader Gorbachev's new program of reform featuring *glasnost* (openness) and *perestroika* (restructuring). The end of communist control of Eastern European countries occurred rapidly in 1989 and 1990. This was followed quickly by significant planned troop reductions in Europe by both superpowers. Expectations were high that the United States and the Soviet Union had come to the end of the Cold War which had made relations between the superpowers difficult for so many years.

A. Michael Dukakis was George Bush's Vice President in 1988.

B. *Glasnost* and *perestroika* were part of the Republican platform in 1988.

C. President Bush promised not to raise taxes and to be watchful of a changing Soviet Union.